FREAK of nurture

essays and stories by

KELLI DUNHAM

TOPSIDE
SIGNATURE
NEW YORK

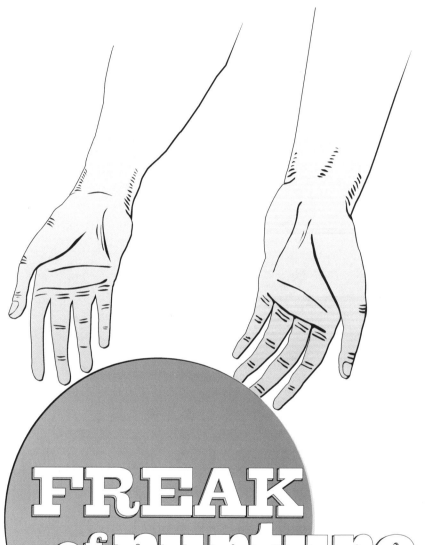

TOPSIDE SIGNATURE
228 Park Avenue South, #14261, New York, NY 10003
topsidesignature.com

Library of Congress Cataloging-in-Publication Data is available.

ISBN   978-0-9832422-8-4   (hardcover)
ISBN   978-1-62729-001-2   (paperback)
ISBN   978-1-62729-002-9   (ebook)

10 9 8 7 6 5 4 3 2 1

First Edition
Cover and interior design by Julie Blair

DEDICATION

This book is dedicated to Eden and Whitney,
my favorite freaks of nurture.

I am so happy you became part of my
strange New York family.

Thank you for all the rice and beans that filled my stomach,
for the long afternoons watching Spongebob Squarepants
that filled me heart.

Thank you for showing me what "hope makes life" looks like.

May we always choose hope together.

Liv sa a se pou Eden ak Whitney (Ruthnie), freak of
nurture-yo m' renmen pase tout lòt freak of nurture-yo.

Kè'm kontan ou te vin yon pati nan
fanmi etranj mwen New York.

Mèsi pou tout diri a ak pwa sa yo ki te plen vant mwen.

Pou apremidi sa yo nou te pase ap gade
sponjbob Squarepants ki te plen kè m'.

Mèsi pou montre'm sa espwa fè lavi ki sanble.

Se pou nou toujou chwazi espwa ansanm.

Contents:

The Adventures of the Grandly and Gloriously Undersupervised

I did not have an unhappy childhood. Instead, I had an interesting childhood, which is quite helpful if your goal is to be a stand-up comic. Or even just a grown-up who has a lot of fun.

One thing that kept my underage years from being an ABC afterschool special was that I was the youngest of seven kids. Not that we are one of those creepy families where all the siblings share both parents. My mom had at least eight, maybe as many as ten, husbands, while my dad had three wives. It was if they each had been told in their formative years that having more than one child with any given partner seriously weakens the gene pool.

I believe that in large families, for each sibling you add, the parents become that much more irrelevant. In a scrawny family that has only two children, the parents, if for some weird reason they are both present, make up fifty percent of the household. By the time my mom birthed me, she made up less than 12.5 percent of the family mass.

I must give my parents credit for some of the ways in which we were incredibly and inexplicably *over*supervised. Our family had a lot of some things (strife, bickering, togetherness, chores, beets) and not enough of others (money, harmony, bikes, free time). My dad grew up on a failing family farm and wanted nothing more than to be a successful businessman for whom farming was a hobby. He became a fan of self-help and self-improvement books, which, in the 70's, were just developing as a full-fledged, if not fully respected, genre.

We were required to sit down for breakfast at 6 a.m., and every day my dad would slam his hand down on the table. He would remind us that Dale Carnegie said, "every man is just about as happy as he makes up his mind he's going to be." I am pretty sure that wasn't a real Dale Carnegie quote, and its meaning was lost on the groggy ten and under crowd.

We were encouraged to read Carnegie's *How to Win Friends and Influence People* as soon as we were cognitively able. My dad would also institute what he called Dale Carnegie Days, usually on rainy Sundays when our sibling bickering was overwhelming. On Dale Carnegie Days if we said or did anything that wasn't in keeping with Carnegie's suggested ways to "win friends" and/or "influence people" we had to go to bed fifteen minutes early for each of the incidents. For example, if we engaged in name calling, being critical, or talking ill of another person who was not present, this would count as one violation.

Once my sister and I got into a yelling fight on a Dale Carnegie Day and our dad didn't intervene but rather sat in the next room, making tic marks as we called each other names like "poopyhead" and "buttface." When we were done, he announced, "Well, I guess you have about twenty minutes to brush your teeth and get your pajamas on." Our fight had earned us a 4:15 p.m. bedtime.

My dad called the TV "the idiot box," and in order to watch our favorite shows we had to first explain how watching each show would help us meet our life goals. It was pretty difficult to make a case that what we learned from watching reruns of *The Munsters* would contribute to any future success. Even if the case was made, in order to earn minutes of TV time we had to spend an equivalent amount of time reading a nonfiction book and present an oral report on the book at the dinner table. We were also required to entertain any questions posed by our parents or siblings.

This is ambitious parenting under any circumstances, but it's unbelievably ambitious parenting for alcoholics.

It was perhaps the alcoholic aspect of the parenting that led to yet another closely supervised activity, something my siblings and I now call Baby's First Drink. There was a minor ritual in our family the first time a kid was allowed to consume alcohol, which took place on each child's fifth birthday. I remember being given a very small glass of watered down lime-flavored vodka the day I turned five. The particular brand must have had some kind of artificial color added because it was bright green. I suppose this is why my parents thought of it as a children's beverage.

My mom later explained it was the French way of doing things. They give their children wine with dinner, and the children think of alcohol as nothing so exciting. Consequently, France has the lowest alcoholism rates in the world. My mom's knowledge of France often revealed itself to be more wikipedia-type truth than encyclopedia-type truth, and I've been unable to verify these claims through the reviews of any standard research. However, at forty-four years of age, I have never been drunk, not even once.

I wouldn't say that the oversupervised hours of my childhood were boring, but the undersupervised days, while technically more dangerous, were also a whole heap of fun.

In Wisconsin we lived with Perry, who also happened to be my biological father. Perry had put together a very extensive wood shop in the back of the barn. One Saturday morning, during the summer after my fourth grade year, I decided that if I could build wings, I most certainly would be able to fly. I located a half-dozen sixteen-inch squares of double-thick plywood and nailed them together in overlapping succession. I used carpet scraps to fashion arm attachments. As an afterthought, I tied a length of bailing twine around my ankle and around a barn pillar because I was not sure how I would get down if I flew as high as I had planned. My brother Ron found me just as I was about to "take off" from the haymow of the barn, thirty feet in the air. He still reminds me he wants 15 percent of whatever I make from my first HBO comedy special, since if it weren't for him I wouldn't be alive to tell this story.

We were not the only undersupervised kids in the area. One mile away, our closest neighbors had a kid my age, who I'll call Henrietta. We were both obsessed with skateboarding. To be more precise, we were obsessed with the way skateboards could be used to catapult us through the air and over objects.

During the summer before eighth grade, we constructed a massive ramp. It was set at a forty-five degree angle and featured a lip made from a two-by-four attached across the top of the ramp. The faster you went up the ramp, the quicker and harder your skateboard would stop when it hit the two-by-four, and the further you would be catapulted into the air. To avoid road rash, we positioned our ramp at the bottom of a hill adjacent to an alfalfa field. The joy of flying through the air—arms flailing, hair flapping in the wind—was only made more precious by the thudding crash at the end.

Soon our unencumbered flying didn't seem particularly challenging, so we started adding items in front of the ramp that we would attempt to clear during our catapult.

We started with coffee cans, but we quickly got bored of them as we could easily knock them over as we flew past. We then filled the coffee cans with rocks and placed them in a pyramid. We were disappointed to find we could still easily clear these, so we started adding farm implements to the top of the obstacle pile. Henrietta had to return to her house when a haying rake left her with a head wound that would not stop bleeding. Her parents halted the fun before we could add more obstacles.

My family moved to Florida the next year, and a whole new world opened up for exploration. That summer my sister Beth and I developed a game we called Heat Inoculation. The premise was pretty simple. At exactly noon, we headed outside to sit in my mom's gray Toyota Tercel in the unshaded blacktop parking lot behind our apartment building, leaving the windows rolled up. Temperatures in Daytona Beach, Florida often topped 105 degrees in August. Each day we tried to beat the record we set the day before for the amount of uninterrupted time spent in the car. The winner of the game was the person who was last to bail out of the Tercel.

That fall my sister was a National Merit Scholarship Semi-finalist. I wonder if she would have been a finalist if she still had the brain cells we baked to death that summer.

It was that same fall that my grandma moved to an Airstream park in southwest Florida. Our entire extended family started celebrating holidays with her. One Christmas, after we had consumed a hearty dinner, the grown ups were fading fast from the effects of booze and tryptophan. It was my sister who first eyed the carcass. "I bet the gators would like that," she said, referring to the alligators that lived in the drainage ditches nearby, and unwittingly starting a family tradition.

Each holiday, after the grown ups were too drunk or distracted to care, we would take the turkey carcass to the edge of the trailer park. Defying the laws of common sense, of nature, and of the state of Florida, we would drop the carcass into the mouths of the waiting reptiles. I would like to say this tradition continued only until we knew better. In fact it continued until the family tradition of heavy drunkenness had passed along to one of my second or third cousins. He had some kind of conviction for underage drinking. As we picked up the carcass, he eyed it warily. "If we get caught," he sighed, "that'd be breaking my probation."

We sat back down. Our tradition was broken, not by fear of being eaten by eight foot reptiles, but by the threat of criminal prosecution.

Much is made of the disadvantages of growing up in a family full of drunks, but little has been written about the obvious benefits. Without the help of the inebriated and inattentive adults treasured blissful memories such as strolling to the drainage ditch, turkey carcass in hand, constructing the apparatus to fly, flying and crashing into sharpened farm tools, could never have happened.

Erasing these moments of danger from my childhood would have no doubt increased my statistical likelihood of reaching adulthood with life and limbs intact. But would I have pursued a career as a comic? When confronted with actual or proverbial cliffs, would I have been much more apt to look rather than leap?

If I hadn't learned the thrill of ridiculous levels of risk, maybe I would have never lived on a houseboat for three years in the urban northeast. Or hitch-hiked across the Dominican Republic so I could do relief work in post-earthquake Haiti. Or scheduled myself on a 1400 mile queer stand-up tour via bus through the rural south. Or converted to Catholicism to try my hand at being a nun.

Perhaps it is my life's calling to start a nonprofit and assist the oversupervised children of today.

"For just twelve dollars a month, just 50 cents a day," a mournful Sally Struthers will say on the infomercial to raise money for the National Association to Let Kids Be Kids, "you can help a child who has been deprived of large omnivorous reptile feeding opportunities."

The camera will pan to a frowning youth, only allowed to play soccer if he is part of an organized team and wearing protective gear.

I will stand alone in an abandoned lot full of trash, rickety playground equipment, and broken glass, like a Pied Piper beckoning the parents.

"Give me your overscheduled children, protected from every danger, thirsting for unstructured time. We will drink unfiltered water and eat non-organic yogurt. We will take the subways and walk, not be carried or driven in an SUV or double-wide strollers. We will pet other people's dogs and not use hand sanitizer. We will have fun."

And the camera will pan away from me and focus on a forlorn pre-teen, who will stand, straddling his bike. His parents will call him back into the house, hand him a helmet and a reflective vest. They will have used safe squishy orange traffic cones to outline the 12-foot square where he is allowed to ride his bike, all well within the confines of their driveway. The camera will close in on his face. He'll shake his head, and a single tear will run down his cheek. He will put on the helmet, buckle the strap and ride his bike slowly and listlessly around his small square.

Sister Mercy Writes
Her Home Letter

This is a transcript of a letter I wrote to my mom while in the convent. We were allowed to write only to our parents, only once a month, so my mom photocopied my letters and passed them along to family and friends. On the upper right hand corner I had written "LDM" with a cross, and Bronx, NY.

FEBRUARY 5, 1995

Hi Mom!

It was good to talk to you today. Thanks so much for calling and for all you have done for me since I have been here. It was good to talk to Grandma too.

Everything here is fine. We are all surviving and trying to be good (easier said than done I guess) and having fun also. The house has been full of visiting sisters. In early December, and then later in January, there was a group of about twenty sisters coming through on their way to India for their home visits.

Mostly these sisters had been stationed in the States and in Latin American, but two of the sisters I knew from Haiti. It was good to see them again. Anyway in early January, Sister Priscilla (one of the oldest sisters who joined when she started the Society in the 1950s) came to visit us. Then all the sisters from all the houses around New York came for Mass, lunch and a nap. We take a nap every afternoon, can you believe it? It's great, like getting to do nursery school all over again and appreciate it this time.

All together, there were eighty sisters in the house. At nap time it looked like a nun bomb exploded. There were nuns sleeping everywhere, including beds, the floor, benches, cupboards, etc.

We have new additions to our community. Two new aspirants came these past two weeks. They seem to be adjusting well to everything and have gotten in the hang of dropping buckets, breaking statues, and spilling soap. It is nice to have the extra sisters now. Our "family" is eight, including our mistress. Because they are doing construction in the Bronx (where the aspirants usually are) we are all together (the aspirants and the pre-aspirants) for now.

Despite the added numbers, we are still having trouble with our singing in the chapel. During adoration, we somehow manage to forget the tunes of the songs we sing, even when we sing the old favorites (*Ave Maria, Salve Regina*) and so then each sister tries desperately to recover the tune (everyone in their own key of course) while the other sisters try not to laugh. In the end, we all end up giggling uncontrollably and have to leave the chapel. We console ourselves by remembering that God has a sense of humor, and He must have a really good one, or I certainly would not be here.

For the last couple of weeks, they have been sending us (that is, 2 pre-aspirants) to Gift of Love a couple of afternoons a week to help out. Gift of Love is a house we have for People With AIDS, so we have a bit of a change of scenery, plus we get to take the subway. Real spiritual motives, huh? The house is really nice and cozy and the number of men living there is limited to less than fifteen, so it really is a family atmosphere.

The other newsworthy item is this project we have going, a 12-step devotional calendar. Using different 12-step books, quotes from Mother, etc., we (aspirants and pre-aspirants) are putting together a little reflection for each day of the year (i.e. each month we use one step). We are trying to incorporate the "I thirst" (the aim of the Society) into the spirituality of the steps. The first step is "I admitted that I am powerless over my own thirst and that my life is unmanageable." The whole "I thirst" thing is just incredible. I know that I went on and on about it in last letter, but the whole idea is really incredible, that God thirsts for us, individually, our own unique love for Him, that we can give it. It's hard to imagine after everything, it just comes back to, "Jesus loves me this I know/for the Bible tells me so."

Well mom, I have no more time so I must go. Thank you again so much for everything. Give my love to everyone. Pray for me, I'm praying for you.

Love,
Sister Mercy/Kelli

Underneath my name I drew "Barfy" a picture of a fish on a skateboard that I had been putting on everything I wrote or made since I was nine years old.

Miracle on Nerd Love Street

I first met Cheryl B in 2005, when I performed at her Atomic Reading Series at a bar in Park Slope. I flirted shamelessly with her but she showed not a flicker of recognition, let alone reciprocity. Several years and many miles later, I saw that she was officially Facebook single and asked her out for coffee. I didn't want to scare her off, since she was so uninterested before, so I left the whole thing very ambiguous. After an unfortunate performing accident, I spent the summer on a friend's couch while wearing a full leg cast. Cheryl came to visit regularly. When I'd complain that I wanted to properly woo her, she'd say, "We're old, I'm happy to sit on the couch with you."

I don't know if I believed in the concept of falling in love, but something sure was happening. She made me laugh, she inspired me to be my better self. Even though we were very different, we fell in nerd love (her words) and became a true nerd unit. I grew up in a farming community in rural Wisconsin. She grew up in an Italian-American enclave on Staten Island. She thought of pasta as a comfort food, while I thought it was something you eat when you don't have any meat left in the house. My signature dish is pot roast. She was a vegetarian.

She was a hilariously cynical, shockingly beautiful woman who learned how to be a queer and how to be an artist in New York. She did an impression of me (in a midwestern accent) that went, "Hi, my name is Kelli Dunham, I'm from Wisconsin, would you like to tell me the worst thing that ever happened to you? Oh and here, have my lunch."

On our first anniversary, we wrote the following re-enactment of our first date.

AT A COFFEE BAR IN THE LOWER EAST SIDE
LATE AFTERNOON

KELLI: Hello there.

CHERYL: How are you?

KELLI: Fine.

[AWKWARD SILENCE]

CHERYL: I see you brought your netbook to our coffee meeting.

KELLI: Yes, I like my new netbook.

CHERYL: I have a netbook too. It's in my purse right now.

KELLI: We are both early adopters I guess.

[AWKWARD SILENCE]

CHERYL: Would you like a drink?

KELLI: No, I have three drinks here.

CHERYL: Oh, yes I see that. Did you bring your own Diet Mountain Dew?

KELLI: Ha ha, I don't drink that much Diet Mountain Dew, no matter what it says on Facebook.

CHERYL: It's funny that we happen to be going to the same queer performance piece at Dixon Place tonight.

KELLI: Yes, quite a coincidence.

CHERYL: We can walk over together.

KELLI: OK.

[AWKWARD SILENCE]

CHERYL: So, how is your comedy career going?

KELLI: Unfortunately, I am not famous yet. How's your poetry career?

CHERYL: I am not famous yet.

[TOGETHER] OH.

CHERYL: You are so funny though.

KELLI: And you are so poetic.

[TOGETHER] THANK YOU.

CHERYL: Shall we head to the venue?

KELLI: Yes, let's.

[AWKWARD SILENCE, WALKING]

CHERYL: Here we are at Dixon Place.

KELLI: Wow, there are so many dykes at this dyke performance art piece.

[TOGETHER] WHAT A COINCIDENCE.

KELLI: Shall we sit together?

CHERYL: Yes, let's. Unless you'd like to sit elsewhere.

[AWKWARD SILENCE, WATCHING SHOW]

CHERYL: My that was a lot of nudity, questions of gender, and references to identity.

KELLI: Yes, I loved it. It was better than *Cats*.

CHERYL: Ha ha. Oh, wait was that a joke?

KELLI: Yes.

[AWKWARD SILENCE]

CHERYL: Let's go to a seedy gay men's bar, even though I am sober and you don't drink.

KELLI: Yes, we will just enjoy the ambiance.

[AWKWARD SILENCE, WALKING]

CHERYL: My, there certainly are a lot of gay men at this gay men's bar.

KELLI: Yes what a coincidence

CHERYL: Let's sit in back in the booth where they show the gay male porn. That would be a good place for two lesbians to hang out.

KELLI: Yes, let's. Unless you'd like to go elsewhere.

CHERYL: No.

[**VERY LONG, VERY AWKWARD SILENCE**]

KELLI: I am going to get a Diet Red Bull. Would you like one as well?

CHERYL: Yes I would like a Diet Red Bull please.

KELLI: There are men here on laptops looking for dates at the gay bar.

CHERYL: They seem very surprised when they come back to this little nook and discover two lesbians.

[**AWKWARD SILENCE**]

[**KISSING AWKWARDLY**]

KELLI: Oh, does this mean we are on a date?

CHERYL: Um, yes, yes I guess so!

Holy Mother of Pride

Mom: [talking about her visit to the Louvre] ....and so I asked the museum guy, "How come all the artists painted Jesus like a sissy?"

Me: Oh. Well what did he say?

Mom: He said, "to show his divinity."

Me: Huh. [Thinking: Whoa, French fags have an answer for everything]

Mom: I don't like that namby pamby Jesus. He was a carpenter! He was strong and muscular and virile!

Since my mom was known to gender police Jesus Christ, perhaps I should not have been so surprised by her response to my coming out.

To express her subtle displeasure at my announcement, she ripped up my birth certificate and sent it to me. This was inconvenient because she destroyed the original certified copy.

When I went to the county vital statistics office to have my birth certificate replaced, the clerk looked at me, then looked at the pieces. My mother was clearly not the first parent to use this method of communication. He then stamped a form that granted me a free expedited replacement.

"We get a lot of that," he said, nodding with his chin at the pieces, "from people who look like you."

I complained to my therapist that my mom was being passive-aggressive.

"No," she corrected, "that's *aggressive* aggressive."

It was hard to reconcile my mother's aggressive aggressive behavior with one particular kindness she showed me twenty years earlier.

Dapper Dan and Dressie Bessie were a set of two dolls, each sold separately and designed to help kids develop the skills they needed to dress themselves. Although both dolls taught the same skills (zippering, buttoning, shoe-tying), Dapper Dan was meant for boys, and Dressie Bessie was meant for girls.

My sister, who is eighteen months older than me, loved getting dressed up, putting ribbons in her hair, playing with dolls and doing every other girly thing in existence. She was given a Dressie Bessie doll.

I, on the other hand, liked my brother's hand-me-down football shirts, wearing a baseball cap backwards, getting really dirty, and doing just about every non-girly thing in existence. When the time came to buy me a "learn how to dress yourself" doll, my mom could have gotten me a Dressie Bessie. But she took a cue from my gender presentation, two decades before the term was even in common queer use, and bought me a Dapper Dan instead.

There was nothing particularly Dapper about Dan. He wore multiple levels of vinyl and a red corduroy vest with huge yellow buttons. Where was he headed dressed like that? Even considering the poor fashion sense that the hapless Dan displayed, I could not have been more pleased with him. I slept with him every night and I kept him until my teen years. By the time I gave Dan up, his face was stained from the frequent nocturnal nosebleeds I suffered, courtesy of the dry Wisconsin winters.

To this day, every time I pull on a pair of men's underwear, I say a silent thank you to Dapper Dan and to my mother.

I had been performing for ten years before my mom saw my comedy act. I perform in a lot of lovely places such as churches, colleges, community centers, coffee shops, and even once at a Buddhist Divinity school. She could have come to any one of those gigs.

In 2009, my mom came with my sister and her kids to visit me in New York and upon hearing that I had a gig when she was in town, declared herself ready to see me perform. Theoretically, if I wanted this story to make sense, I'd explain what had changed between me and my mom. The only problem with that is I don't know. More than a decade had passed since the birth certificate incident. Was it time healing all wounds? Watching the Ellen show every afternoon? Some kind of religious experience?

At any rate, "ready" might have been overstating it a bit, but resignation is close to ready.

At least alphabetically.

She had decided to come see me at the Stonewall Inn, in the middle of June, on the fortieth anniversary of the eponymous riot. I was opening for Lynnee Breedlove, founder of the dyke punk band Tribe 8, at a show hosted by sexpert and radio personality Diana Cage. It was a swirling vortex of never ending gayness, and I had brought my mother to the eye of the rainbow-tinted hurricane.

The show started with Diana musing about her deep abiding love for her big huge vagina.

My mom whispered to me, "Are all lesbians so proud of their big huge vaginas?"

I whispered back, "I'm not sure mom, that might just be Diana. She's had a lot of stuff in hers." *

My mom nodded wisely, as if that was the very answer she was expecting.

---

* It's okay to say this about Diana because I'm pretty sure she identifies as a person who has had a lot of stuff in her vagina.

I had opened for Lynnee in the past. The show Lynnee had been touring at that time involved Lynnee holding up a number of small adorable stuffed animals and having them talking softly about their chosen identity, e.g. "I may look like a teddy bear, but I identify as a pig." The show my mother attended began with Lynnee strolling on stage wearing nothing but a strap-on.

Lynnee then spent the better part of an hour talking about, handling, and chopping up different phallic objects. The show culminated with a standing urination demonstration. My mother and I were in the front row, less than a foot away from the stage. It was intimate.

My mom sat very still through this, and not once did I even see her flinch. Hoping to generate alcoholic amnesia, I heard myself say, for the first and only time in my life, "Could someone go get my mom another glass of wine."

I put my arm around her and said, "I don't really get performance art all that much either."

When the show was over, every queer in the place rushed over to meet my mom, who many of them had heard stories about from my performances. They fussed over her and told her she was amazing. She and Diana talked shoes, and my mom and Lynnee gave each other a huge bear hug, as if they had both been waiting their entire life for just that moment.

One friend gave my mom a personal guided tour of the bar and the surrounding area. He had been one of the men arrested and released the night of the original riots. "It's a little bit like being shown around Buckingham Palace by the Queen," I told her, thanking him.

He corrected me, "It is *exactly* like being shown around the Palace by the Queen."

My mom was gracious. She smiled and hugged the entire room of queers like they were old friends.

I was entertained by her pop quiz around the breakfast table the next morning.

The first question was about an older friend who had been kind enough to give us a ride home from the show. She asked, "Is Tim *normal?*"

"Well he's partnered with a dyke in a chaste domestic partnership and he will have kinky sex with pretty much anyone who will have sex with him. I don't think gender even enters into the equation of who he plays with."

By "normal" my mom meant heterosexual but all my information didn't actually get her any closer to the answer.

Then she asked, "So Lynnee is a woman who lives as a man?"

I hemmed and hawed for ten minutes before realizing the honest answer was "I don't know." My mom went on to ask a stupendous number of questions about wardrobe, which seemed to be the most perplexing aspect of the whole super queer evening for her.

"So the one person...who was sitting next to us...uh... dresses like a woman, but the person...the woman...the... other person...whose lap she was on...dresses like a man? Is that always the way it is?"

My sixteen year old nephew replied, "Not necessarily Grandma Piper. Role playing and role identity are often two different things."

"Where did he learn that?" I asked my girlfriend later.

"My best guess? Dungeons and Dragons."

There was one more question that my mom meant to ask, that she wanted to ask, but that she felt embarrassed to bring up. Finally, I said to her, "Out with it, Mom," and she swallowed hard and began.

"Well Kelli, I was wondering, in your subculture,"

I didn't even know my mom knew the word subculture.

"Yes, mom?"

"In your subculture, are you um, are you considered um, are you, um, *attractive?*"

"Indeed," I said to her, with a slight head motion towards my beautiful girlfriend, who had just come back from walking the dog, "there are some women who want nothing more in the world than to date someone who looks just like me."

The year after my first partner died, my stepdad was sent home from the hospital under the auspices of hospice care. His diagnosis seemed to be old age, years of alcoholism, hydrocephalus caused by World War II shrapnel pressing on his spinal canal, and possibly "some cancer." This is the level of information my mother was capable of conveying at the time.

When some people develop dementia, they usually forget what year it is, where they live, or the names of their children. Not The Colonel. He forgot that he was an asshole, probably because he also forgot where the scotch was. I flew down to help my mom with caregiving arrangements and was stunned by his sudden kindness. He told me twice that he was proud of me, that he loved my new haircut, and that he was so glad I came to visit.

It seemed unlikely that The Colonel would make it to Christmas, so we put the tree up early for him. He was too confused by then to follow even a sitcom on television so he would ask my mom to turn everything off in the living room, except the tree, and he gazed appreciatively at the multicolored lights.

"That's a helluva tree, Nance," he'd say to my mom, sometimes as often as once an hour, "you did a superb job. It's a helluva tree."

After The Colonel went to bed each night, my mom and I sat together in the living room and talked about his illness and brainstorm ways of making sure she had all the help she needed. Comparing notes, we found that loving a very ill retired army colonel and a very ill burlesque diva were not such different experiences.

Each morning I'd go into my mom's bedroom, plop on her bed and watch while she did her makeup. She fussed over her appearance despite intense caregiving fatigue. I wanted to promise her that it would all be okay, but I knew it wouldn't, so I just sat on her bed and made small talk.

The Colonel died a few days before Christmas. When neighbors stopped by with food, my mom introduced me with, "Kelli lost her spouse this year too. Heather died of ovarian cancer in February."

There is a woman who used to live in my house with my siblings and our father, and then there is my mom. They look remarkably similar, one just has a few more wrinkles. But they act nothing alike.

I made my mom a silly grief guide from a black-and-white speckled composition notebook. Inside I pasted cartoons, photos of cute animals and dubiously helpful suggestions like, "Affirmations don't have to be ambitious to be useful. 'Just for today, I will get out of bed' is a great start."

In the very early morning hours of December 27, my mom sat drinking her third cup of coffee. I donned a green blanket and said, "I will now do the traditional dance done on the fifth morning after a death in the family." Covering myself in the bedding, I jumped around while singing the Ramones song "I Wanna Be Sedated." I crashed into the kitchen wall, crawled back into the living room. I then re-emerged wearing a different colored blanket and announced, "I will now do the traditional dance after the death of the last born in a family following the traditional green blanket dance."

My mom laughed until coffee came out of her nose.

And this is a how a sad queer and her sad mom came to sit together in a Florida living room at 5:34 a.m.
We watched a CSPAN Book TV special on the origins of swearing.
And then we discussed the benefits and drawbacks of periods of sexual abstinence.
I drank my Diet Mountain Dew.
My mom sipped her coffee.
We were both strangely comforted.

The ABCs Of Adventures In Gender

First, a few words about gender.

That's totally a joke. No queer person for the last fifteen years has ever said just a few words about gender. But when people ask me, "Are you a boy...or a girl?" I am reminded of Lynnee Breedlove's brilliant response "What are you asking me for? Does it look like I know?"

Part of this is gender stinginess. You can't be greedy and have a little of each gender, there's only two and you have to pick one! Haven't you ever heard of gender-warming? You have to pick one or by the year 2022 we're going to be completely! out! of! gender!

Would that it were so.

I don't know if people ever get my gender right, since I have no idea what it would look like for them to get my gender wrong. However, if they decide I'm male, they do underestimate my age by an average of 2.7 decades.

Age? Eh. Gender? Whatever. I'm not picky. Just accurately assess my phylum, genus and species and I have no real complaints.

A is for *Argument* One fine spring day when I was living in Philadelphia, I was walking along the Delaware River path on the way to my apartment. I was singing a happy song, like I do sometimes, especially when I have a brand new haircut that I particularly like. I walked by two older, grandmotherly looking women standing together.

WOMAN #1 (CALLING OUT TO ME): Hey, whaddya have to be so happy about?

ME: Huh? [split second passes while I try to decide if I am going to tell her about my haircut]

WOMAN #1: I mean, what are you even? A man? A woman?

ME: I guess either one, maybe that's what I'm so happy about.

WOMAN #1: Silence. [She was clearly not expecting an answer].

WOMAN #2 TO WOMAN #1: I told you to leave him alone.

WOMAN #1: Leave her alone.

WOMAN #2: He

WOMAN #1: She.

WOMAN #2 (LOUDER): He!

WOMAN #1 (LOUDER STILL): She!!

WOMAN #2 (QUITE A BIT LOUDER): He!!!

I don't know how much longer they went on like that, because I yelled "enjoy the lovely day" over my shoulder and kept walking home.

B is for *Blank Slate* A few years ago, I was in Atlantic City to celebrate my best friend's birthday. We stayed at the Borgata casino. You know who was playing at the Borgata that weekend? Clay Aiken.

Before we left for the Casino, I used hair gel and donned a pink oxford shirt, two things I don't usually do but which apparently, alter my physical appearance in some kind of significant way.

Perhaps it is particular feature of Atlantic City that people are required by law to pay absolutely no attention to detail. So maybe my next CD will be called *I am NOT Clay Aiken*, featuring the tracks will *No Seriously I'm not Kidding, I'm Not!* and *Hey! Why are These Old Ladies Trying to Touch Me?*

Small children have mistaken me for Eminem. Adult comics like to refer to me as "Lance, from the Backstreet Boys." Or was it the New Kids on the Block?

I am like a science fiction character with no real appearance of my own, so that folks can project whatever they'd like to see onto me. Is this creepy or a gift from the universe? It's so hard to decide sometimes.

B is also for *Bathroom* When I had a home visiting job, I seldom used the bathroom at my clients' houses, mostly because I felt like it was intrusive. But one afternoon I was desperate and made an exception.

Unfortunately, my client didn't tell her baby's father that I was using the bathroom and the lock didn't work that well. He walked in on me while I was sitting on the toilet. I had a long shirt on and he got out of there pretty damn quick so it was not as bad as it could have been.

As I finished up and was walking around the corner from the living room, I heard the dude saying, "Yeah, I can't believe her thighs are so thick for such a scrawny thing." The client's grandmother replied, "Well, I can't believe she pees sitting down." By the time I realized they were talking about me, I had already walked smack dab into the middle of the conversation. Luckily, this was at the end of the visit so I smiled and said, "I guess we've gotten to know each other a little better today."

C is for Cars People are always yelling strange things at me out car windows.

One time a dude pulled up in an old school Trans Am, rolled down his window, and bellowed, "FAT BOY ON A DIET DON'T EVEN TRY IT!"

Which left me with more than a few questions.

What's with the rhyming heckles?

Had he been waiting his whole life to say that?

And if so, how sad.

Also, what made him think I was on a diet?

Did I look hungry and crabby?

So many questions.

D is for Decoding I told the *Fat Boy On A Diet* story for quite a while as part of my act. One night a teenager explained, "Those words are from a '90s rap song."

"Oh," I said, "that explains perfectly why that random person yelled them randomly at me."

E is for Everyone's A Comic I went with my ex Cassendre to see a movie. Cassendre walked up to the counter to buy the tickets. I was a step behind her, fooling around with my phone. The dude at the counter looked at us and said "one adult, one child?"

Cassendre laughed really hard. She then explained that she had adopted me. "It's a new reverse celebrity thing, black people adopting white babies. Or sometimes even grown folks." The person behind the counter wasn't amused.

F is for Faggot Not too long ago, I was walking down the street and a middle-aged guy shot over his shoulder at me: "Faggot."

"Well, *this* is a teachable moment," I thought.

"Hey actually, 'faggot' is a negative epithet customarily

used for male homosexuals—that is, men whose primary sexual and emotional attraction is to other men. I am a cisgender female, and therefore the more appropriate negative epithet for me would be 'dyke,' that's spelled D-Y-K-E. However, because I am on the genderqueer spectrum and some people would consider me a boi, that is a B-O-I... Hey, dude, where you going?"

Whatever. He started it.

G is for *Government* A few years ago, United States Senator Arlen Specter came to the health center where I worked. It was a big press event, I believe he had come to take credit for something. He shook all my co-workers' hands but when he came to me, he clapped my back and said, "Good to see you son." At the time, I was dressed for work and wearing a professional ID.

My co-workers thought this was hilarious and so began good-naturally calling me "Son." When I (not so brilliantly) mentioned that I had been compared to Macaulay Culkin they adopted that name as well. All the time. Even in meetings.

"Let's ask Macaulay about that."

H is for *Home Alone* One of the new interns thought that my actual name was actually, for real, Macaulay Culkin. I guess she had never seen *Home Alone*.

The longer it went on, the more awkward it would have been to correct her, so I didn't. Finally, one day she referred to me as "Macaulay" to the Dean of the college affiliated with our health center. When the Dean didn't know who she was talking about she said, "You know, Macaulay Culkin."

The Dean had seen *Home Alone*.

And that was really awkward.

I is for **I Am Not My Own Son** My first two books were published by an academic press, and my editor and I had mostly an email relationship. One day I needed to stop into the office to pick up a package of illustrations I was supposed to look over. When I got home I found it wasn't what I needed.

I called my editor who said, "Oh, I was expecting to hear from you, the receptionist said she handed your son the wrong package."

I was silent for a minute because I didn't know what to say to that.

What could I say? "I am not my own son?" It sounds like a self-help message, something Oprah might come up with.

So I just said "Oh."

J is for **Just Go Along With It** And in that moment of indecision I created a teenage son that I never had. It's very convenient to have a fake teenage son.

I blame everything on him. Trying to avoid a conference call? Sorry, I had to pick my son up at soccer practice.

K is for **Kelli Sue** My mom named me Kelli Sue, which is proof positive that if you go far enough into the midwest, you're actually in the south. I didn't like the Sue part of the Kelli Sue very much, so when I was seven I started telling people my name was Kelli Sam.

It was amazing how quickly my mom was willing to compromise on dropping the "Sue" part. No one but my great Aunt Marilyn calls me Kelli Sue anymore.

L is for **Lost Child** One Saturday morning when I was living in Portland, I went with some friends to a huge rummage sale event at the Portland Expo Center. It was a fundraiser for an expensive private school.

The other folks in the rummaging contingent had a much higher tolerance for shopping than I did. Mid-morning I sat down in one of the overstuffed chairs that was for sale, pulled a juice box and a mini bag of pretzels out of my backpack, and proceeded to take a rest and have myself a little snack.

I was interrupted by a helpful volunteer who wanted to direct me to the "lost parents" station.

When I said "pardon me?" He realized, well, at least that I wasn't a lost child.

And he tripped over his tongue apologizing and almost tripped over his feet trying to get away.

M is for *Mom's Choice* It's one thing to be mis-gendered when you're hanging with your friends and co-workers. It's another thing entirely to have this experience in front of your parental units.

When my mom broke her hip and was in rehab, one of the other residents complimented her on the helpfulness of her "sweet grandson."

The person continued on for fifteen minutes about how this gave her hope for the youth of today, and my mom didn't have the heart to correct her.

N is for *Not Quite Ready for Daytime* The publisher for my kids' books assigned me a freelance publicist named Abby, a freelance publicist who would be named Muffy if it were still the 80's. Abby's voice always went up at the end of her sentences, even her declarative sentences.

Abby tried to get me booked on *The Bonnie Hunt Show*. The junior producer loved me, and so after a successful conference call, I was talking with Abby on the phone.

"Kelli, do you have a video you could send them?" asked Abby, as a double question, since she had constructed an interrogative sentence, and because her voice always went up at the end of her sentences.

I said "Abby, do you know what I look like?"

"I'm googling you right now."

"Oh my."

My physical appearance is apparently shocking enough to make a 24-year-old person use the phrase "oh my."

O is for Oh No She Didn't Abby sent my photo to *The Bonnie Hunt Show*. She called me two days later with their reply, "They need something where you're looking a little more normal," she said.

P is for Pitching. Bad pitching. "So, Abby," I said, "you pitched me to a visual medium without seeing a photo of me first?" I was asking a question. My voice did not go up at the end.

I made the Bonnie Hunt people a video in which I was looking very "normal," sitting in a rocking chair and wearing a red gingham dress. I sent it directly to the show, bypassing Abby completely.

"So I got a weird call from *The Bonnie Hunt Show*," said Abby, less than twenty-four hours later, "they said something about your video being... creepy?"

P is also for Prom When I had a job that involved working with teenage girls in their homes, every spring I had the same difficulty.

Inevitably, a client would be talking about prom, disappear for a moment, saying, "I'll be right back," and then reappear carrying her dress.

I don't know anything about prom dresses. I smiled and nodded, and said things like, "Oh yes, that's nice," and make other vaguely positive comments, but often the girls would be looking for actual feedback. One client showed me a book of 200 swatches of fabric and went through each one, asking me what I thought of them. As far as I could see, they were all the same color: blue.

Making conversation about prom dresses is not really something boi-dykes should do unsupervised.

Eventually I realized I needed assistance, and so I cranked up the bat signal and pleaded for help from my femme friends. I printed some of their suggestions on index cards and memorized:

Where did you get the shoes?
How are you going to wear your hair?
That's an amazing shade of (whatever color).
That's really beautiful. What is your date's tux like?
That's a really pretty shade. I love that material.
What jewelry are you going to wear with it?

Q is for *Queen of Confusion* One lovely summer day, two friends I call my dyke moms invited me to go swimming with them at a pool club they belong to in South Jersey.

All afternoon I'd been looking at the diving board and thinking, "It'd be really fun to go off the diving board." I hadn't jumped off a board in a long time. This is partly because diving boards are somewhat rare in public pools these days, due to liability concerns. It also partly because adults do not jump off diving boards unless they are training for the Olympics.

I couldn't stop thinking, "I want to go off the damn diving board." I waited until there weren't too many kids around and got in line.

As I climbed the ladder, I heard the kid behind me gasp.

"Oh my god, she's a grown up."

And then kid behind him said, "No, he's not."

R is for *Right Answer* During a spontaneous arts and crafts session, at a queer conference in a decidedly big chain hotel, a friend made a crown out of paper which did not fit her head. It did fit mine, so she gave it to me.

I wore it around for the rest of the night, because, hey, she gave me a crown. It's not every day that someone gives me a crown. This worked out fine when I was in the confines of the conference programming. However, I forgot, and I was wearing it in the elevator when I ran up to my room. This led to the following interaction:

> **LITTLE KID IN ELEVATOR [TO HIS MOM]:** Why is that little boy wearing a crown?
>
> **MOM [EYES ME, QUIZZICALLY, CLEARLY EXPECTING ME TO ANSWER]**
>
> **ME [PRETENDING TO TEXT MESSAGE SOMEONE]:** Silence.
> **MOM:** Um, I think he's in a school play.

S is for *Sir Ma'am* Have you ever been sir ma'amed? Someone's helping you in a store and they say, "Thank you very much, sir."

"Sir. Ma'am. Uh, Sir! I mean Ma'am. Uh I mean—Oh."

It's more fun when you don't rescue someone in the throes of Sir Ma'am Panic. Just wink, smile, and say, "It's one of the mysteries of modern life," and go on with your day.

S is also for *Suggestions* One night I was on the subway coming home and some kids were talking loudly and bumping into each other near me. One turned to the other and said, "Quit it, you're going to make me bump into that...lady...or um whatever."

And so suggested a possible new gender identity for me. "Um, whatever."

T is for *Twins* In the land of queer, apparently everyone looks alike. The Atlanta Hyatt has a 24-hour store where they sell both Krispy Kreme donuts and Diet Mountain Dew. I was out all day performing at Atlanta Pride, had returned late to the hotel, and was buying some of each. I had the following conversation with the cashier:

CASHIER: Wait, did you...do you have a twin? Here?

ME: No, no, um. No.

CASHIER: Wow, there was someone who looks just like you here. But the tattoos and piercings are different.

ME: Well, there a lot of people who look like me here this weekend.

CASHIER: Are you having a convention?

ME: Kind of. Like a convention. It's gay pride.

U is for *Understandable* I've noticed while I'm on tour that for each mile I go away from a big city, my gender becomes closer to male and my age drops precipitously.

I shouldn't have been surprised when the clerk at a convenience store somewhere in rural Virginia handed me the number for a runaway hotline along with my Diet Mountain Dew. It would help, I suppose, if I wore my ball cap frontwards, or drank a beverage more frequently consumed by adults, but what's the fun in that?

V is for *Very Random* A friend was visiting me from out of town and late one Friday night he decided he wanted to go out for a cheesesteak. We walked around my neighborhood, the bars had just closed and the sidewalks were overflowing with drunken frat boys. My friend was calling it "straight pride."

As we passed The Irish Pub, one dude said to me, "You look like the little brother of my first pussy."

Whatever the hell that meant.

W is for **Women's Room** One afternoon I decided that since I really needed to use a bathroom, I would do so in a very touristy hotel around Times Square. A man came into the bathroom after me, because he saw me going in, and assumed it was the men's room.

I heard some women shooing him out. So after he left, while I was doing my business, I heard the same two women talking about how terrible it was that there were, "two men in the women's room."

And I thought, "Wow, I can't believe *two* guys followed me in here." When I walked out of the stall and saw their faces, it became clear that I was the second man in the women's room.

I was reminded of that Sesame Street book with Grover. He's worried about the monster at the end of the book, until he gets to the end of the book and realizes *he* is the monster at the end of the book.

X is for **Xenophobia** I went out to the suburbs to work with the recording dude on edits for my new CD. He had a mobile studio van parked behind his house and he told me to meet him there. As I stepped into the van, his neighbor came rushing over with her two dogs. When she saw me, she stared for a minute and then saw Recording Dude, to whom she said, "We've had juvenile delinquents starting fires behind our yard so I saw the back pack and I thought he's not from around here..."

I just smiled and didn't contribute anything to the awkward silence. After she sputtered for a while she left and I told the recording dude we should call this next CD *I Am NOT a Juvenile Delinquent.*

He explained that his neighbor was a bit of a right wing wackado. I noticed he left the door open and the sound up while we edited, so she got to hear fisting jokes all afternoon.

Y is for *Yowza* I found out that a photo was stolen from my website and was being used for verbal target practice on a Ford trucks discussion forum.

"Yowza!" said one poster. "That thing looks like Dave Matthews with boobs. "

I'm not a pop culture wiz, so I did a Google image search for Dave Matthews.

You know what?

I kinda *do* look like Dave Matthews with boobs.

Z is for *Zebra* When I was hunting around a thrift store looking for clothing to wear while performing, I came across a lovely Victoria's Secret shirt/pajama top type thing. It was barely worn and what did I have to lose but my two bucks and ninety-five cents? True, it was black with pink stripes but I am secure enough in my masculinity to wear such a garment.

I was using my almost-lingerie striped shirt as one of my costume changes for pride gigs. After one all day pouring rain pride event I didn't take my striped shirt off when I left the stage because it was cold and I didn't want to lose the extra layer of warmth that it provided me no matter how small.

When we stopped at a turnpike rest-stop, I got out to use the bathroom and to my surprise, no one gave me a hard time, screamed or ran out thinking they were in the wrong bathroom.

The shirt is a lightweight synthetic and folds into almost nothing. It has become my Portable Gender Marker Garment and I can quickly don it for potentially dicey bathroom situations. Who knew that lingerie was the key to peeing in peace?

Sarah Palin,
an Artificial Plant,
Fascination with Church
Ladies, and Me

"God is good, all the time."
  —*Popular American saying*

If I believed in God at this point, perhaps I'd agree with the first part of that popular American saying, "God is good." I couldn't get behind "all the time" because some kids get a pony, and some kids get leukemia.

Since I was a wee little queer, I've been like a ninth grade band geek who has a crush on a God who is the captain of the varsity football team.

Can't He just notice me?

Why doesn't He notice me?

Look, I learned all about football and memorized the playbook. Why doesn't He like me yet?

This lopsided relationship started in my early years. I grew up evangelical Christian and went to church on Sunday morning, Sunday night, and Wednesday night. There was plenty of time to memorize the playbook. The fact that I started out Born Again confuses people who know that I am an ex-Roman Catholic sister. I had to convert to Catholicism to become a nun. You can't get this fucked up with just one of the world's major religions. I would have tried Buddhism too, if every white lesbian in America hadn't beaten me to it.

When I was in kindergarten I came home from Sunday School and told my mom about learning the Bible verse Matthew 17:20, "I tell you the truth, if you had faith even as small as a mustard seed, you could say to this mountain, 'Move from here to there,' and it would move. Nothing would be impossible."

My mom listened as I tearfully informed her that I didn't even has as much faith as a mustard seed because I told the hill behind our house to move and it didn't. She responded with the all-purpose and pragmatic theological truism, "Well, maybe it wasn't God's will."

God's Will is the evangelical Christian's "Get God out of Jail Free" card. It can be used to explain all the places Christianity contradicts itself within the text of the Bible, and wherever Christianity conflicts with reality. For example, as a kid I was taught that the fossil evidence of evolution had been created by God specifically to challenge our faith in the truth of the Biblical story of creation. Even our questioning was God's Will.

God's Will is a handy concept. If you believe in God's Will, whenever you are faced with a phenomenon that makes no sense, whether it's something endlessly tragic like the Holocaust or something endlessly irritating like always picking the slowest supermarket line, you neatly affix the God's Will label on it, and it all makes sense again.

The only drawback of this Everything Is God's Will business is it makes God look like a giant flaming asshole. Worshiping someone who has an unpredictable temper and erratic judgment is not easy. This may partly explain why some types of Christians have their political tighty-whities in a wad on such a regular basis.

As ludicrous a tool as God's Will is, I miss it. I long for a secular equivalent of God's Will just as I sometimes long for a God of my own. I imagine most atheists relegate the nonexistence of God into the same category as the nonexistence of the Tooth Fairy, Easter Bunny, or Santa Claus. Not me. I take the nonexistence of God much more personally. To overwork the relationship analogy, it's as if God is one of my more difficult exes. He is someone with whom I really wanted to connect, someone I wanted to spend the rest of my life with. Alas, we were never able to work it out.

My difficult relationship with this Diety I Don't Believe In is further complicated by my actual relationship with some of his followers. People who love Jesus, as a group, have not been very nice to homosexuals. However, as individuals, people who love Jesus have been extremely kind to this homosexual.

Because I have a good number of these good Christians in my past, I accept Facebook requests from people I knew at any period in my life. These are friends I went on mission trips with in the 80's, fellow nuns, Bible College classmates, and the first guy I ever kissed who is now sporting a non-ironic mullet. Like queers, Christians often create a middle username for Facebook that advertises their beliefs. My queer friends sport names like Steve Equality Diamond or Amanda Marriageforall Smith, while the Christians create monikers like Pam Jesuslovesyou Wheeling or Kate Prayerbackinschools Turner.

Having Kate Prayerbackinschools Turner and her like-minded souls as Facebook friends makes for interesting reading, since so many evangelical Christians use their status updates to talk directly to God. Kate writes, "Dear Lord, I thank you for my two handsome responsible sons. Please keep them safe as they travel to their soccer tournament and help them glorify You, win or lose."

Directly under this post on my news feed I see, "Steve Equality Diamond is attending the Deep Dick Collective."

This online information exchange reaches well beyond Facebook. I recently received an email from Stephen Elliott, the social studies teacher from the small Christian high school I attended. He was mainly writing because he was "offended" by my use of the word "podunk" as a substitution for the actual proper name of the school on my website. I quite honestly thought I was doing them a favor. Would they really want one of the top five hits for a "Warner Christian Academy" Google search to be Warner's most backslid student, a queer atheist stand up comic living in Brooklyn?

Mr. Elliott began his email, "Hello, Kelli, I was reading about your successes and I was a little surprised but not totally," and then took me to task for what I had written about Warner on my site. I spent forty-five minutes crafting what I now know was a ludicrous reply, replete with sentences like, "I think we both could agree that the Warner dress code at the time when I attended strictly enforced the rigid gender binary."

My girlfriend asked me, "Why do you even care?"

It took me some serious head scratching to figure it out. I cared because they cared. The school guidance counselor once wrote me a three-page note about how she saw me mature in my ninth grade year. The English teacher my senior year spent hours helping me refine my writing skills, and she also taught me how to temper my verbal obnoxiousness. My volleyball coach gave me tips on how to get along with my mom better. My softball coach's husband taught me how to drive a stick on their lime green Volkswagen Bug. The whole school helped me raise money to go on mission trips where I learned that there was more in the world than just me and my problems. Not to mention the music teacher, who was also the music minister at the church I attended. His wife invited me over to babysit one day and I essentially parked my ass on their couch and stayed until I was grown.

These were not the only Christians who have helped me through a tough spot. When I moved to Miami shortly after Hurricane Andrew, the one apartment I could find was microscopic, covered in black mold, and full of mice. Occasionally when you flushed the toilet, anything in the bowl would spray up through the shower drain so hard that it would splash on the ceiling.

My older sister A.N. lived ninety minutes away from Miami. When I told her about the apartment, she got a babysitter for her two young children, bought $100 worth of heavy-duty cleaning supplies, and fought rush hour traffic through three South Florida counties to come help me de-hovel my place. We cleaned for no less than six hours. When she left, my tiny dump was spotless.

A.N. is a conservative Christian and, at that time, was an active participant in the fundamentalist boycott of Disney for not actively discouraging Gay Days.

The same person who was boycotting a mainstream business for passively supporting the LGBT community helped me clean poo from my bathroom ceiling. So perhaps I can be forgiven my extreme ambivalence with evangelical Christianity?

Although I don't know exactly who I would be seeking forgiveness from.

Because I feel so ambivalent about the Christians I know personally, I'm similarly fascinated with how Christianity manifests itself in pop culture and politics. I am thus equally obsessed with, although perhaps slightly less ambivalent towards, televangelists and Jesus-based far right-wing political efforts.

My favorite televangelist is the Queen of Evangelical Self-Help, Joyce Meyers. I watch her show every day at

6 a.m. and her full-on bananas talk makes me shudder in horror and quiver in anticipation. Perhaps I shouldn't admit this, but watching Joyce Meyer while I sip my first Diet Mountain Dew of the day is also deeply soothing to me. I love the upbeat if somewhat directive, "It's time to start enjoying everyday life," theme song. I love the message of freedom from the "demons" of co-dependence, and I love that she openly has a face lift every few years and tells people to "just get over it" because she's on television, after all.

My mom once gave me a whole set of Joyce Meyer tapes called *Eat and Stay Thin* which promised to "restore a healthy balance in your life by letting Joyce reveal to you biblical revelations exposing common misconceptions regarding weight control." That was the same year she gave me a copy of the *The Weight Loss Bible: The Bible for People Who Want to Lose Weight* in which the author exhorted the reader to only eat foods mentioned in the Good Book. I guess the theory is that after five days of loaves and fishes for breakfast and sacrificial lamb for lunch and dinner, you'd be too bored to overeat. I still have that book, it's right next to *Help Lord, the Devil Wants Me Fat*, a gift from my mom when I was a teenager.

But all that crazy self-help Christianity isn't even a tenth as entertaining as the escapades of some of the more politically-involved Born Again Christians. My search for this Theological Twilight Zone is how I ended up on a recent southern tour taking a pit stop in Birmingham, Alabama with Sarah Palin.

I was on a comedy tour of the rural South, and as part of that tour I had signed up to be a volunteer with the Extraordinary Women Conference, a fundamentalist Christian women's gathering sponsored by the Million Moms. The queers usually know the Million Moms as the Million Moms against Ellen, but they've had their knickers in a knot over a lot of "godless media" sins: girl on girl kissing in the Urban Outfitter's catalog, the Sports Illustrated Swimming Suit Issue, and Mattel considering a Kardashian Barbie Doll line. They send out emails about every ten days, imploring their constituents to complain directly to the sponsors of evil, godless, pro-homosexuality, and pro-sex television.

I'm particularly charmed by the Million Moms' email campaign against a Liquid-Plumr ad which they object to because the manufacturer is "trying to sell products with sex." Their complaint? A commercial shows "a man in the produce section standing beside cucumbers with a price sign behind him reading sixty-nine cents." I agree someone in this situation is obsessed with sex, but it doesn't seem to be the Liquid-Plumr people.

The American Family Association created The Million Moms as an allegedly grassroots initiative, although there's a dude at the helm who I am pretty sure doesn't identify as a mom. A Million Moms, at the standard statistical shorthand, would have 100,000 queer offspring. If their emailing habits are any indication, they are not being very nice to those kids. So I decided that someone needs to talk to these moms, on their turf, and I decided that someone should be me.

My friends and my therapist were all confused by this plan. Was I going to do some direct action? By myself, of course not, no. A demonstration of one is a lonely thing indeed. Was I trying to gather fundamentalist Christian trade secrets? What trade secrets? They point to the Bible and say, "We believe *that*." Was I going to create some kind of comical mass disruption? Nope.

I was just going to attend, help out by volunteering, and if anyone engaged me in conversation, I'd answer honesty about why I was there.

What could go wrong?

Well, my wardrobe for one thing. What does a big queer wear to a fundamentalist Christian conference anyway? After a number of mishaps, I've finally learned the difficult lesson that the harder I try to look straight, the gayer I appear. This was brought home to me several years ago when I showed up for a trip to meet my girlfriend's mom wearing an outfit I had picked out just for the occasion.

"Well, that's an interesting choice," my tactful girlfriend said, as she looked down at my clothing: a light pink v-neck sweater, black jeans, and matching pink Vans. I explained, "I was trying to look you know, less dyke-y." This sent my normally reserved girlfriend into such guffaws that she stood in the middle of Port Authority with tears from laughter cascading down her face.

Trying to avoid just such a scene with hundreds of strangers, I went for an understated choice, an Old Navy American Flag t-shirt. I felt like the character in *The Birdcage*, defending his decision to place Playboy Magazines in the restrooms for the straight people. "What? It's what they like."

The second thing that could go wrong was my volunteer assignment. I talked on the phone with Heather, the Extraordinary Women's volunteer coordinator, who also could have been mistaken for the perkiest human alive. She thought I belonged on the greeting committee, since "those folks are the very first friendly faces people see when they walk in the door of the conference."

When I showed up in person and Heather got a look at me, she nonchalantly reassigned me to the "floater" position. I wouldn't want my face to be the first face people see at a Christian women's conference either. Unless it were a queer Christian's women conference, which would probably not fill up the Birmingham Convention Center.

Unfortunately, my floater position was to staff the speakers' sales table, a position that could have easily resulted in my spending sixteen hours taking people's money and handing them one of Sarah Palin's hardcover classics. This seemed to be over a random philosophical line that even I could not cross. So I did what any mature, intelligent human would do on such an occasion. I ran behind a large artificial plant and hid until the volunteer meeting was over.

There is something about spending forty-five minutes stooped down behind an artificial tree at the volunteer meeting for a Christian women's fundamentalist's conference. It really gets you thinking about where your life is going. Luckily, I had anticipated potential problems with my volunteer position. To make sure I could get in, I had purchased a basic level ticket for the conference. Just the ticket that cost fifty bucks, mind you, not the 250 dollar pass that allowed all access to the events, special seating, a meet and greet with Sarah Palin and the opportunity to wear a pink ID that said "Palin" on it.

It was on entering the Birmingham Convention Center arena for the first time that I realized another problem with my plan: the math. There were 7,000 of them and one of me. I listened to that Dar Williams song with the "I'm Not Afraid of Women" refrain on my iPhone while I huddled in the bathroom. It took me fifteen minutes to muster up the courage to come out.

I found a seat and watched the women as they listened to the first speaker. Thus began my very long weekend. There were few surprises since I quite obviously know this culture. I have an underlined Bible and my real name is Kelli Sue. I looked around me and saw my people, although I was unsure if when they looked at me they felt the same.

I talked with lots of people, and did some listening as well. I'm not sure I changed anyone's mind about anything, but at least people could say they'd met a real live queer once if anyone asked them at a church potluck. No one was anything but nice, although one particular conversation illustrates the whole experience.

I was sitting with Church Lady X in the lobby of the hotel attached to the convention center. We were both eating Subway sandwiches because it was the only thing in the area that was not overcooked hot dogs. We chatted about the relative merits of different sandwich combinations and then the subject turned to (surprise, surprise) God. She gave me her testimony* and then asked about me. I launched into a ten minute explanation of why I was there, my history, my plan and a little bit about the comedy tour I was on.

Her eyes glazed over. My guess what that she was scanning her mental hard drive for previous experiences with open queers at conservative evangelical conferences that she could draw on to formulate a response.

When I stopped talking she responded with all she had to give me. "You're looking for Jesus then?"

I smiled, nodding, and said, "I guess we're all looking for our own Jesus," and got up to throw our trash away.

The event ended with Sarah Palin's much-anticipated keynote speech. I could not believe the welcome those women gave her. Picture a '90s Ani DiFranco concert, times one-hundred, and you'd be nearing the same female excitement level.

Women yelled, "We love you Sarah" throughout her speech. What is it about Sarah Palin? Why does she have to be so...hot?

I had a seat just off the left side of the stage. The whole time she was spouting off her own special brand of

---

* the story of how she found Jesus

paranoid political insanity I kept looking at her legs and thinking, "That woman needs to have sex with me."

My guess is that's not what the other 6,999 Extraordinary Women were thinking.

On the way out, I ran into Church Lady X again. We greeted each other with a hug. As we walked out, she tapped the back of my Audre Lorde Project 25th anniversary sweatshirt. On the back it reads, "We are strong because we have survived — Audre Lorde".

"We are strong because of Jesus," Church Lady X said, whispering into my ear.

I stopped for a moment. Those were not quite fighting words, but they were close. I growled in what I hoped was a semi-friendly way.

"Don't mess with our Audre and we won't mess with your Jesus," I said. Her eyes again glazed over again but she nodded yes.

I put my arm around her shoulders, and I walked her to her car.

You Know Who Does Anal

The money for my nursing school education came from two very different sources. The first was a scholarship from the Theresa M. MaKenzie Memorial Scholar Fund, a living trust administered by Extremely Rich People. The second was my night job at a low-demand homeless shelter.

The MaKenzie Memorial Trust was a scholarship given through my college that was initially based on standardized test scores. If you did well on a nursing school admissions test, the Dean of students would bring you in for an interview. It was a very confusing interview because there were no questions. At the interview I was provided only with a series of grooming tips on how I should appear when I went to interview with Extremely Rich People who administered the MaKenzie Trust and were the real decision makers. Based on the tips I got from the Dean, I could conclude they were completely obsessed with the idea of a "dignified personal appearance" of each of the MaKenzie Scholars. It is one of the seven wonders of the modern world that the Dean didn't take one look at me, a chubby genderqueer ex-nun with a very bad haircut and an unfortunate proclivity for cargo pants, and suggest I send a stunt double for the interview.

I sat on a chair in the Very Helpful Dean's office for nearly ninety minutes, taking notes about what I would need to do to look "presentable." I think what I needed to be presentable was a completely new body, a standard issue feminine gender identity, and perhaps a personal history that didn't involve quite so much farm work as a child, but her coaching was designed to help me build a temporary detour around all that. She even told me which store would have a good price on a "skirt outfit" in my size. I had never worn anything remotely resembling an outfit in my life, unless you count my matching sailor shirt and pants in first grade.

The Very Helpful Dean's final advice before I took leave of her office was that I should make quite certain to wear stockings to the interview. Since I was only familiar with the term "stockings" in reference to Christmas, I must have looked confused. She quickly clarified, "I mean, you know, pantyhose." I would like to say there is no way I would have shown up to meet the Extremely Rich People wearing a skirt outfit and white fur-lined red Christmas stockings, with perhaps my name embroidered on the cuff. I would like to say that, but I think it would be giving my 24-year-old baby dyke self entirely too much credit. I'm sure it never even occurred to her to tell me that I should shave my legs before I put on the pantyhose, since it also never occurred to me to do so.

I showed up for the interview with the Extremely Rich People with my leg hairs sticking out like porcupine quills through my pantyhose, and the price tag for my skirt outfit (which I bought on the way to the interview) still firmly adhered to the backside of my skirt. I didn't discover the tag until forty minutes after the interview was over but I considered it lucky, since I hoped to return the skirt outfit to the store.

Perhaps I confused The Extremely Rich People. Perhaps I charmed them with my rapier wit. Perhaps they felt sorry for me because I looked like I had been dressed by Minnie Pearl. In the end, I got the scholarship. The nice thing about them being Extremely Rich was that it was an Extremely Generous scholarship that covered all tuition and fees. I took a job working nights at a low-demand homeless shelter to cover my living expenses.

A low-demand shelter is exactly what it sounds like, which is to say that it is a shelter in which the demands on the facility's residents are very low. For example, many shelters require that residents refrain from using drugs or alcohol in their facility, and that the residents take their prescribed psychiatric medications. This shelter had no such regulations even though most of the women who stayed there had issues with severe mental illness and substance abuse. Most of these homeless women were extremely vulnerable on the street and also regularly caused a general ruckus wherever they went in downtown Philadelphia. The city funded the shelter to try and prevent the latter, but as staff we were primarily worried about the former.

On my first night staffing the shelter alone, I witnessed a resident named Teresa taking advantage of a quiet moment in the living room to prepare for her last heroin shot of the day.

I looked at her and cocked my head.

"You can't shoot up in the living room."

"They said there weren't any rules here."

"Well, there's not a lot of rules here, but there are some."

"Show me where in the rule book it says that," she said, calling my bluff.

I looked through the policy and procedure three-ring binder kept on the front desk. There wasn't a "no shooting up in the living room" rule. Still, I thought it was a good policy.

I conceded.

"Well, okay it's not a rule. But I think you shouldn't shoot up in the living room." I was still floundering, "Because, um, it's an illegal activity and, um, I'm not supposed to see it."

I had a brainstorm. "It's not fair to the other women." I meant it's not fair to the other women who might be in recovery, but that's not how Teresa understood it.

"It's not my fault if they're all out of smack." But then she reconsidered, "Damn, you'll probably make me share."

As if *that* was in the rule book.

A few days later Teresa came back to the shelter extremely mad about an unrelated incident and swinging a two-by-four. I could see her through the closed circuit TV and refused to let her in.

She shouted at me through the little black intercom box using every expletive in the English language and a few I am quite certain she was making up.

"You can't come into the shelter swinging a two-by-four," I said, mustering up all the authority and what I hoped was street cred that my two weeks working at the shelter had earned me.

Teresa wasn't having it.

"I know there isn't a rule about that."

She was getting louder, threatening to wake everyone in the shelter. That wouldn't have been a pretty sight. I sputtered into the intercom.

"No, it's not a rule but you can't come into the shelter swinging a two-by-four because you are bigger and stronger and tougher than me and you don't need the two-by-four to kick my ass." This logic clicked with Teresa. I watched through the monitor as she tucked the wood between a dumpster and the side of the building and returned to the door. I let her in, she patted me on the head and went directly to bed.

Over time, I grew to enjoy the women who lived at the shelter and cherish that job. When everyone went to sleep I studied for my nursing school exams. Plus, the relationships were honest. The women didn't have to pretend to not be using drugs and I didn't have to pretend not to notice they were high.

Sometimes one of the women would be unable to sleep and would come sit across from me while I studied. They'd talk about their lives, where things went wrong, and where things went right. They'd ask me questions about my childhood in rural Wisconsin or what my friends or apartment or classes were like. I'd try to find disgusting pictures in my nursing textbooks and shove the book across the table to gross out the person I was chatting with. I started bringing my dermatology book each night since the entire middle section was dedicated to glossy color photographs of all the revolting things that can grow on human skin.

The person staffing the shelter on the 7 p.m. to 8 a.m. shift was required to make breakfast. This was mostly an easy task, warming up pastries or putting out cold cereal and making sure the coffee was ready when the women started to wake up. On weekends, the shelter manager would put eggs on the menu. The women all got up at different times and it was impossible to keep the eggs warm, so I started cooking eggs to order. It was humbling how much the women appreciated this simple gesture.

In the evenings the staff person on duty was supposed to sit at the front desk in order to be able to quickly let residents in the front door and to keep out anyone swinging a two-by-four.

Next to the desk was a pay phone for resident use which some of the women would use to conduct their business. As staff we felt ambivalent about the shelter-provided pay phone being used to negotiate sex work. On one hand, it was technically illegal. We were always concerned that the shelter would be run out of the neighborhood. On the other hand, we definitely didn't want women constantly running in and out or having their clients knocking on the door of the shelter.

One evening it was particularly busy and Teresa was answering the phone and brokering the calls. Maybe she was testing me or maybe her feet were just tired, but she insisted on yelling the requests into the living room.

"Hey, who wants to work tonight?" or "Shelly, you busy later on?"

I looked at her over my books.

"I'm right here. I can hear you," I told her.

She yelled again, but more quietly.

The evening wore on, and I gave up the battle after I had secured a promise from Teresa that she would stop answering the phone when the lights went off at 11 p.m. Less than thirty minutes later, just as I began checking over the log to find out what I was supposed to be making for the next morning's breakfast, I heard Teresa's voice, louder than she had been all evening.

"Linda,Whitney, Renee...which one of you guys takes it up the ass?"

I stood up. In the homeless shelter sex work hierarchy, those who take it up the ass are usually pretty far gone and really desperate.

I yelled back at Teresa, matching her decibel for decibel.

"You can't just take fifteen steps into the living room and ask quietly?" I said, as if I was suddenly the Emily Post of the shelter world. "C'mon, you know who does anal!"

Every woman in the shelter heard me. Every woman in the shelter thought it was the most ludicrous thing a human being has ever said in all of recorded history. The laughter spread from the living room into the dorm, rising, then falling, then rising again. Each time that it seemed like the ridiculousness of what I had said spent itself, one of the women would repeat, "You know who does anal," in Midwestern white person voice that supposed to sound like me. The cycle would repeat itself.

The laughter didn't last just that night. Wherever I went in downtown Philadelphia, shopping, going out to eat, attempting to romance my latest crush, if I ran into one of the women from the shelter I'd hear, "You know who does anal," followed by uproarious laughter.

It was a strange form of celebrity.

For my nursing school graduation, the women at the shelter did an amazing thing. They all chipped in and made me a dress. The dress looked like it had been made by a dozen drug-addicted women with severe untreated mental illness living in a low-demand shelter, because it was. Renee, the administrator of the dress, called it a "classic A line." It was mainly blue, except the back, where they had run out of blue material and used green instead. Part of the hem was finished with mint dental floss. I thought it was beautiful.

I wore that dress to my nursing school graduation because if a dozen drug-addicted women with severe untreated mental illness living in a low-demand shelter get together and make you a dress, you are required by the laws of ethics, etiquette and human decency to wear it. Also, the women from the shelter had all invited themselves to my nursing school graduation.

I couldn't have been more proud as I walked across the stage in my all-homeless designer dress to receive my

Bachelor's of Science in nursing. As I reached over to shake the University President's hand, I heard cheering and laughter and twelve voices above the others.

"You know who does anal!"

Because they were twelve women yelling in a crowd of five hundred, I hoped that most people at the graduation could not make out the words of my special congratulatory greeting.

When I went to shake the hands of The Extremely Rich People, who always attended the school graduations, one of them said, "Were those women yelling *you know who does—*" and then she stopped. I suppose that's not a sentence that Extremely Rich People who care about things like pantyhose and looking ladylike get to say very often.

I waited, hoping my silence would force her into finishing.

She sputtered, "Well you have very interesting friends."

I smiled, proudly, and said, "Yes, yes, I do."

Does It Take More Than Duct Tape to Be a Dyke?

I loved my first job as a nurse, but sometimes going to work was a bit hard on my butch ego because I was continually out-dyked by the straight women there. I worked with two women who are *honorary* lesbians. Meaning they were not lesbians in the "primary emotional and sexual relationships are usually with women" sense but rather in the "give me ten minutes and a tool belt and I can fix anything" sense.

Case in point, I noticed two of my coworkers had a particularly bad cases of poison ivy. I asked co-worker #1 where she might have gotten it. Perhaps while working outdoors? She thought briefly. Finally she said, "I haven't been doing anything really out of the ordinary. I suppose I could have gotten it when I cleared a path through the woods around the house. I was in a hurry because I only had Sunday afternoon to reroute all our septic lines."

"You're rerouting the septic line?" I asked. "I'm not quite sure whether to be impressed or call 911."

"Well Kelli," she said in a tone of voice you might use when talking to someone who has just suffered a stroke and whose cognitive abilities you are not quite sure of, "you can't expect me to call someone for help every time I have some little project to do."

At that point co-worker #2 walked in the door. I didn't have time to ask about her outdoor activities because we had some important business to attend to.

Me: I'm glad you are here, I'm not sure but I think the toilet is broken. It's spraying pink water all over the walls and playing a dance mix version "Nobody Knows the Trouble I've Seen"

Co-Worker #2: Really? Sounds interesting." She headed into the bathroom, rolling up her sleeves. She was dressed in a business suit and carried only a roll of duct tape and short length of IV tubing. Five minutes later she returned, wiping her hands on a paper towel.

Me: So, do you think you can fix it?

Co-Worker #2: (Simultaneously opening her mail, checking her messages on her cell phone and drilling holes in the wall so we can hang up a lovely framed photo essay that depicts great influenza outbreaks of 20th century) "Hmmm, oh it's working fine now. In fact, I think we can even use it to convert that PC health education software so we can use it on those donated Macs. "

At that point, I dropped the discussion. I was looking for the user's manual for the paper clips and I didn't need any honorary lesbians distracting me.

Bad Habit

Have you ever had a bad habit? A really bad habit. I'm not talking about leaving the toilet seat up, fingernail nibbling or inserting Q-Tips into the ear canal. That's amateur stuff.

To me, a bad habit, a *really* bad habit, is a behavior that makes you wake up in the morning and say "I can't believe I did that, again, what was I thinking?"

We all have a friend who consistently chooses the absolute worst job for their situation. For instance, Mary Jane hates, hates, hates the cold. She's the kind of person who could be standing on the very surface of the sun, rubbing her arms and muttering, "I wish someone would turn the goddamn heat up around here."

So what job does Mary Jane take? She works in a sub-freezing laboratory logging the mating rituals of Alaskan penguins. For overtime, Mary Jane drags herself over to the equally freezing lab next door to help Consumer Reports test the efficiency of winter camping gear. Mary Jane now suffers from stomach ulcers and migraine headaches but isn't quite sure why.

Yeah, what was she thinking?

And doesn't everyone have that friend who always picks inappropriate people to go out with?

My mom is a perfect example of this phenomenon. She has been married more than a half dozen times. She managed to handpick not one, but a number of alcoholic men. What was she thinking?

"Hmm, now let's see, my last five marriages to alcoholics ended in financial ruin, emotional chaos, and the disintegration of my entire nuclear family. But you know, I've finally found the right alcoholic, I know it will work out this time."

Soon, when things get rocky, she is philosophical, explaining that, "There's more than life than being happy y'know."

It's hard to argue with logic like that. There's also more to life than breathing, but breathing seems like a good place to start.

Why have I proclaimed myself the world's foremost authority on bad habits? I don't have the market cornered, but as a big genderqueer dyke and former nun, I've had to answer the "What were you thinking?" question more than a few times.

It's been a while since I was a nun, but you'd be surprised by how often my sordid past comes back to haunt me.

For example, I had an overnight liaison with a cute chick I had met snowboarding. The next morning as she was finishing brushing her teeth, she said, "Hey, did you know you say the Hail Mary in your sleep?" This was news to me.

I said, "I don't suppose by any chance you found that sexy?"

She didn't answer.

When the average queer person finds out I used to be a nun, I get a predictable set of questions.

I know I gave up a significant portion of my life to live in the bowels of the Catholic Church, the institution voted "Most Likely to Keep the Patriarchy Alive and Well" the past one thousand years running. But I was convinced that I had what the Catholic Church calls, "a vocation to the religious life." Only for me this meant, "a desire to recreate my dysfunctional family of origin in an adult context."

People still ask:

"Did you know you were gay?"
—Uh, yeah I suppose so. I own a mirror.

"Haven't you ever listened to the Pope? He's a raving homophobe!"
—Of course I know the stance of the Catholic Church on homosexuality.

"So what then? Were you high on Twinkies?"
—Nope.

"Hot for nuns?"
—Um...

"Kidnapped?"
"Alien abducted and then anally probed?"
"Out of your fucking mind?"

I've been asked "why" like this, so often, I've honed down my response to a 3.4 second sound bite. "I was looking for a life that made sense."

At the time in my life when I first encountered the Missionaries of Charity, their way of life made perfect sense to me. The Missionaries of Charity (known as MCs) are not the matching-shoes-and-pocketbook, theater-going, theoretical-poverty-loving sisters common in the American Catholic Church today.

The MCs are good old-fashioned nuns. They're exceptionally strict, even by nun standards, and they interpret their vows of poverty, chastity and obedience in an almost breath-takingly literal way.

Strangely enough, this didn't scare me, maybe because I grew up in an irregularly religious home. My mom was an ecclesiastical chameleon. She adopted the church-going habits of her husband of the week. I knew the basics. I could tell the difference between a Baptist and a blowfish and a Catholic and a carburetor. Still, I was the religious equivalent of the personal ad designation "bi-poly-curious" and was really open to trying anything that helped life make more sense.

I was surrounded by overwhelming poverty. I often thought of the money I had spent in Pavlovian response to Madison Avenue drivel. But the MCs were different. When E.F. Hutton talks, these sisters don't listen. They don't care how "finger-licking good" KFC claims to be, and they certainly don't look to McDonald's to provide their food, friends and fun. Since they don't take wage-earning jobs, they don't pay taxes into the coffers of any country's military-industrial complex.

The MCs are a part of a grassroots effort to help provide food, shelter, and medical care for those who don't have it. In stark contrast to many in the religious world who seem to have Ph.Ds in rationalizing, the MCs have this crazy idea that Jesus wasn't joking when he said "feed the hungry."

In a kind of interpersonal revolutionary gesture, the MCs live in communities made of women from many different cultures who dwell together peacefully.

These characteristics appealed to my sense of idealism. But they also appealed to my sense of guilt.

I first met the Missionaries of Charity while doing volunteer work in Port-au-Prince, Haiti. I don't think most people would say I lived a sheltered life until that point.

I grew up in an area of Wisconsin where no one cared about drunk driving laws because everyone just took the tractor to the bar. In my town, domestic violence was considered less of a social problem and more of an athletic event.

Whatever the difficultly I saw or lived as a child in rural Wisconsin, it was different than watching people starve. It was different than seeing kids die of infections that fifty-seven cents worth of antibiotics could fix. It was different than a first-hand look at the chaos and poverty that centuries of racism, colonialism and self-serving US policy had wrought.

As an American in Haiti, guilt quickly became my breakfast, lunch, and dinner.

Perhaps I thought that maybe, just maybe, a life with the MCs would reduce it to more manageable mid-afternoon snack size.

When I met the MCs, I was volunteering full-time in Port-au-Prince at a school for kids with disabilities.

One morning as I was eating breakfast in the communal dining room, Dr. Rich, an American dentist who also worked at the school, said, "Hey, I'm going to the Home for the Dying. You wanna come along?"

"Home for the Dying?" I tried to act casual. "Sounds like a fun place." I considered the proposition as I stirred my coffee.

The students at our school had been sent to their homes in the provinces because of political problems in the Port-au-Prince, so I was very bored. And I was just a little curious. I was also still enough of an adolescent to interpret Dr. Rich's question as a challenge, and I said yes for the sake of pride.

"What the hell," I thought, "if it's too much, I'll just turn around and go home."

Just a short walk later, we were ushered into the Home for the Dying.

"Good morning, sister," Dr. Rich said, just as I caught a glimpse of a short, slight woman in a floor length habit and checkered apron.

I grabbed his arm and mouthed, almost frantically, "This place is run by nuns. You didn't mention anything about nuns."

My mind raced, trying to review what I knew about correct behavior when meeting a religious sister. Do I kiss her ring? No, that's for a priest or the pope or something. Do I curtsy? I was beginning to panic. Do I say bless you? Probably only if she sneezes.

Dr. Rich laughed at my expression. "Relax, Kelli," he said, gently trying to pry his arm out of my death grip. "They're just people."

Turning around, I got my first full look at a Missionary of Charity nun.

True to Dr. Rich's word, she did indeed seem to be "just a person." But she was also a woman, and an exceptionally beautiful one at that. The nun smiled at me and said, "Oh Jesus must have known we needed extra help today. We are behind with the regular work because we have been so busy laying the foundation for the new morgue."

She then, with one easy motion, shifted the sixty-pound bag of concrete she was carrying from one shoulder onto the other shoulder so that she could more easily take my hand.

She smiled at me again and said, "Welcome."

Sigh.

My little guilt-ridden but immediately crushed-out ass stayed and worked that whole day. And I went to help out the next day. And the next. And the next. The political chaos didn't end as quickly as hoped, and so the kids didn't return until the next school year.

By the summer, I was in love.

Not with Sister Mary Concrete Carrier, or any single

Missionary of Charity. I was in love with all of them. Everything about them made me swoon.

I loved their white habits.

I loved the way they moved so silently on the stairs.

I loved watching them plan and work together.

I loved working along beside them in hard manual labor they undertook with almost frightening intensity. And I also loved the way this same manual labor left their forearms well-muscled and entirely lickable.

I didn't want to watch this from the outside. I wanted to be an insider in this very passionate club. I hoped I had what the nuns referred to as a vocation, or calling, to be an MC. I volunteered with the nuns in Haiti, and also in Norristown, Pennsylvania and finally, Miami.

After four years of volunteering, the top brass at the Missionaries of Charity gave me permission to report to their convent in the South Bronx for aspirancy, the first level of training.

By that time, I thought I knew all there was to know about the MCs. As it turns out, I did know all about the work they did, but practically nothing of their lives inside the convent.

The week before I was to leave for New York the sisters from the Miami MCs invited me for tea. They had hand-printed a sign on notebook paper and taped it above the entrance to the convent.

It read, "Welcome Home Sister Kelli."

It was very sweet. They also made me a card that was just as heart-felt, but not nearly so heart-warming.

The sister who handed the card to me urged, "Read it aloud."

I started, "Our dearest Kelli. You have a beautiful vocation. To be a faithful wife of our crucified spouse will hurt, and your heart will be pierced just as they pierced the heart of our precious Lord. Your love of Jesus must destroy you completely."

Destroy was written in all capital letters with several exclamation points added for additional emphasis.

I gulped.

Another sister asked, "See the little red smudges? Do you know what they are?"

There was red ink dripping out of each rounded letter. I was afraid to even ask.

"We drew in the blood of Jesus!"

All six nuns around the table looked at me expectantly. They had clearly spent a lot of time making the perfect card.

"Thank you, sisters. It's certainly very," I thought for a very long moment, "intense."

They beamed.

On some level I was taking all this in a quiet panic, but sitting in the nuns' refectory, I realized I felt very much at home. Coming from a crazy alcoholic family and not having had much therapy, perhaps I should have thought twice about making a major life decision because it felt "like home" to me.

Regardless, I felt quite hopeful as I climbed the steps into the red brick convent in New York. Once inside, I met my group sisters who were also beginning their training, as well as our aspirant mistress, Sister Milagro. Sister Milagro had the unenviable task of molding us into brides of Christ in the manner required by the MCs. She quickly apprised us of Missionary of Charity rule #1:

Holiness comes only through suffering.

"Any time you have a chance to make things a bit more difficult for yourself you should do so," she said. "Your own selfish, lazy nature will only make you evil."

This was her way of welcoming us with light friendly conversation our first night at dinner.

Wanting to be faithful to the ideals that had prompted our entry into the convent, my group sisters and I tried desperately to make things more difficult for ourselves. But whenever we tried to choose what Sister Milagro called "holy inconvenience," we almost always found that following the guidelines of MC life beat us to it.

We washed our hair only once a week and only in cold water with whatever kind of bar soap had been donated in the previous few days. Although we spent hours performing manual labor, we didn't afford ourselves the odor-absorbing benefits of deodorant. Even in the sticky South Bronx summer we didn't use fans or even open the windows. We used pages torn from the phone book as toilet paper. Further along in our training we didn't use toilet paper at all.

Jesus rejoiced in our soiled discomfort.

I wondered sometimes what we must have looked and smelled like to the folks who came to eat in the soup kitchen where we were working. Whenever we joked about how smelly we were, Sister Milagro would say something like, "It's beautiful, no? Such a blessing to help with chastity."

I supposed it might well have helped with chastity, but it couldn't have helped the appetites of any of the folks who had to be within whiffing distance of our armpits while they ate.

As time went on, Sister Milagro explained that I was guilty of having insufficient docility when I was corrected. "The voice of your Mistress is the voice of God in all things but sin," she said. But too often I found that what the voice of our Mistress was telling us to do wasn't exactly sinful, it was just stupid. All the same, I would try my best to comply.

Sometimes we would return home from working in the soup kitchen and Sister Milagro would greet us with a big smile and announce, "Today, sisters, because we love Jesus, we are moving the dorm into the dining room and the dining room into the dorm." As we looked at her in stunned silence, she'd add, "Soon, sisters, soon."

Sister Milagro would wait and search our faces for any sign of an emotional reaction. Sometimes I would manage to smile and say, "Yes sister, thank you sister," which was the only acceptable verbal response. Even if I managed the smile and the Vulcan-like reply, I would still commit the heinous sin, Sister Milagro said, of walking away like my shoulders were angry.

In order to embrace our own suffering, Sister Milagro insisted that we meditate on the sufferings of Jesus. Holy Week, the week in which Roman Catholics everywhere obsess about Jesus' torture and death on the cross, provided a convenient opportunity to do this. MC Holy Week is like a trip to Disneyworld, if Disneyworld had been designed by Marquis de Sade.

We spent our time in penance and listening to endless and gruesome recitations about the crucifixion. We recited the Stations of the Cross morning and night, each time starting with, "Jesus is condemned to die/God through sin I crucify."

I agreed that Jesus being killed was very bad. But I didn't see why we had to hear about it in such revolting and graphic detail.

During Holy Week we constantly chanted the Chaplet of the Divine Mercy, which involves saying "for the sake of his sorrowful passion" no less than fifty times. We were supposed to be remembering that Jesus died because of our sins, each of our individual sins.

It seemed both devastatingly depressing and hopelessly codependent to me. If a friend saved your life by grabbing you out of the street just as a speeding car almost ran you down, you'd be plenty grateful. But what if that same friend demanded you verbally acknowledge that fact a couple dozen times every day? What if they insisted you dedicate a special week to thinking about nothing other than that moment when they grabbed you? After a while you'd hate your friend. After a few years of that you might even wish they had let you take your chances on street. At least you would have wanted to know in advance what the expectation was.

We also spent Holy Week cleaning our already spotless convent. As we scrubbed the underside of a sink with a toothbrush, wiped imaginary dust from the door jambs, and disinfected the ceilings, Sister Milagro would ask, "When we see things are neat and orderly, what does it remind us of?"

It reminded me of obsessive-compulsive disorder, but it turns out the right answer was "God."

I was continually confused by Sister Milagro's questioning. It felt like I was the perpetual losing contestant on a *Who Wants To Be A Living Saint* game show. In retrospect, I would have done okay if I'd learned to rotate three answers: "God," "the Virgin Mary," and "because I suck as a human being."

Holy Week was also when we were introduced to the book *True Devotion to Mary*, which is a book designed especially to pulverize self esteem. One section reads, "We are all more evil than serpents, more stubborn than donkeys, more stupid than oxen, more slothful than pigs." Sister Milagro shared this portion with us in chapel one night and I fell over laughing. Something about the random animal comparisons and the bizarreness of the ritual just struck me as funny. Who said are oxen are stupid? By whose measure? Of course, the harder I tried not to laugh, the harder I laughed, and then my other group sisters started to laugh, and then we were all shaking with silent giggles.

So after asking what was so funny, Sister Milagro just
threw up her hands and said, "Very well sisters, just go to
bed. You will not be able to keep Jesus company tonight."
We were supposed to be having all night adoration of
the Blessing Sacrament and, as usual, we were exhausted.
As I brushed my teeth, I thought, "That certainly worked
out well."

New surprises came every day, each more unpleasant
than the last. Especially memorable was the morning Sister
Milagro lectured us that if we really loved Jesus we should
mortify ourselves by using the bathroom no more than once
a day. This seemed so ludicrous to me, I thought she must
be kidding. So I started to laugh. She was not amused by
my reaction. She was even less amused when she overheard
me whispering, "Great. Just call me Sister Mary Bladder
Infection."

Another rather unsavory surprise came as a result of the
time we spent in the chapel. We knelt for prayer on the
bare concrete floor for three hours and forty-five minutes
each day. Because of this, we developed oozing calluses
on our knees which would stick to our habits when we
knelt, rip open when we got up, and begin oozing again.
We explained to our mistress how this was wreaking havoc
with our laundry, which we washed by hand. She pointed
to the crucifix. "What wound do you think you are making
in Jesus' tender flesh when you complain about spending
time with him?"

My response might have been a tad sarcastic.

"Oh, sister those wounds aren't from us. All those
wounds were already there. I guess they were made by the
sisters who had so little love for Jesus that they went to the
bathroom twice today."

Sister Milagro threw up her hands. She told me I knew
nothing about mortifying my carnal, fleshly desires. I told

her no, I was completely mortified, every time a visit to the bathroom left me with the New York phone listings Swanson through Swinton transferred onto my rear end.

One morning we came back from working at the soup kitchen to find a miniature leather flogger and a bracelet made of barbed wire placed on each of our lunch plates. Sister Milagro explained that we were to use the flogger on ourselves every Friday before bed, and we would wear the bracelet every morning on our upper arm from the time we got up until after mass.

"These practices," she explained, "will help with chastity."

I bit my tongue almost clear through trying to keep from saying, "Oh is that what they're calling it these days?"

A large part of convent life was Finding Out There Were More Things To Do Wrong Than I Had Ever Known. Every day at noon and then during night prayers, we were supposed to do an examination of conscience. We were supposed to figure out what we did wrong and write it down in a little book so we could confess it, or work on it, or feel guilty about it. Preferably, we would do all three. To accompany our own little book we were given a book called The Examination of Conscience. In it were lists of things we might have done wrong. And in case you hadn't actually done anything wrong, a lot of the lists were annotated with possible wrong motivations for doing the right thing. I asked my aspirant mistress why there wasn't a space for doing the wrong thing with the right motive. She told me not to be so fresh.

Some things we might have done wrong (transcribed exactly from the book):

Do I make the resolution to control my tongue from getting dirty *(p5)*

Do I realize how much of an affect my angry words have

on my Sister? (like the one bite of Adam of Eve that has affected all mankind) *(p4)*

Do I help a Sister struggling with her bucket? *(p8)*

Do I conquer my temper? If not, I don't love God even for one minute? *(p15)*

Am I so ugly or preoccupied that I have no time to allow the Sisters to love me? *(p16)*

Do I spoil Mother's name by my words and actions? *(p17)*

Am I selfish in being moody? Do I know that moodiness is devilish pride in action? That it comes from a soul, which is not of prayer? That it is a curse *(p20)*

Do I use my tongue for the good of others? *(p32)*

Through all this craziness, I was hoping the process I was going through would make me holy since joy was in short supply. It was not just my mom's words now, it was God himself saying, "There's more to life than being happy you know!" But I stayed on, encouraged by the occasional glimpse of beauty I saw in our life.

For example, the day after Easter, all the MCs in the New York area got together for a picnic. Sister Carmel and I found a basketball and we walked around to different clusters of nuns, recruiting them for a pick-up game. When let loose on the basketball court, the nuns transformed into women who run with wolves. Sister Beth, who had been the first American sister to join the MCs, wore thick glasses and usually moved with slow, heavy steps. When I put up my hands the first time to block her jump shot she feigned fright. "Please Sister Mercy, you're scaring me."

Five minutes later, I attempted to shoot from near the free throw line. She sailed through the air and slapped the shot right back in my face. Her fingernails grazed the inside of my hand. "Ooooh sister Mercy," she giggled, taking my hand in hers, "are you okay?" And then, "Oh my goodness," looking more closely at my bleeding palm, "you have the stigmata!"

Sister Maria Juanita, a very young, very small sister from Columbia claimed she had never played basketball before, but she shrugged and said "It's beautiful to try, no?"

When Sister Carmel attempted to pass the ball to another sister on her team, Sister Juanita appeared from out of nowhere, slapped the ball loose, dribbled once behind her back, and passed the ball to her team's point guard. Sister Carmel stood with her hands on her hips.

"I thought you said you never played basketball before!" she yelled down the court.

"Oh maybe a little," Sister Juanita said, eyes sparkling, "maybe defense."

At the time, Sister Manno was the oldest living MC outside of India, and she had survived three open heart surgeries. She ripped the ball out of the hands of a much younger sister and proceeded to run up the court. When another sister accidentally stepped on the end of her habit, Sister Manno continued to run for the lay-up. When she turned around, triumphantly having scored two points for her team, she was wearing only her long skirt-like undergarment. Our collective cry went up, "Sister!"

She smiled and began to re-dress. "I made the basket, didn't I?"

In my letter home the next week, I wrote three pages about the game and concluded, "I guess the sisters play basketball the way they do everything else. With their whole hearts."

These types of moments were rare. In general, we spent every minute scrutinizing our actions for selfish motives, or engaging in some type of manual labor or self-flagellation. I guess the idea was that if we just worked hard, and hated ourselves enough, we wouldn't have much time or energy for any particular friendships.

"Particular friendship" is the convent euphemism for nun-on-nun action. The measures they took to prevent this type of behavior bordered on ludicrous. We were exhausted. We smelled awful. We wore multiple layers of complicated clothes. At 4:40 a.m. it was completely dark when the first bell of the morning rang to wake us, but we could only get dressed after we had pulled the top sheet completely clear of our respective beds and each nun had created a makeshift tent to cover every single one of our sexy body parts. Even our hands were supposed to be under the sheet.

At that time of morning, I wasn't having a lucid thought, let alone a lusty one.

But all this BDSM practice and rhetoric eventually had an effect on me. Especially when coupled with the constant and close proximity to these other tough-ass nuns, united by a deep purpose and living life on the most basic level I found I was as horny as a repressed baby dyke in a convent.

When we were supposed to be meditating I'd be imagining a very fey Jesus wearing a pink chiffon scarf in addition to his hipster sandals and white robe and fucking me up the ass with only spit for lube. One of Sister Milagro's favorite lunch table conversations was, "How did you experience Jesus this morning in meditation sisters?" I was always stuck for an answer. Jesus was supposed to be our spouse, but I was fairly certain that didn't include unlimited rim jobs with a bonus round from God incarnate.

One day when I was cleaning the upstairs bathrooms in the part of the convent that was used a homeless shelter, I got quite a surprise. I was bent over the tub, scrubbing it with a tiny bit of steel wool and the lye and Ajax combination that the nuns swore by, although it was lethal to both lungs and skin.

Sister Maria Shanista appeared, leaned over me, and

whispered "Where is it? The woman's one."

I stopped scrubbing.

"The woman's one?"

She pointed to an area near the middle of her body. At first I thought she was gesturing to the large crucifix the professed sisters all wore tucked into their waistband. But then she added, "People touch it," she said, "and it feels nice?"

I didn't want to admit that I had been touching mine to make it feel nice every spare moment I had since I'd walked in the convent doors. Sometimes even during the fifteen-minute nap we took every afternoon. Even though we slept in a collective dorm with beds merely inches apart, I huddled under my seven blankets and believed that no one was the wiser.

I nodded.

"That's a mortal sin," Sister Shanista whispered.

I wasn't sure if she was accusing me or asking me. One convent rule was that we were supposed to pray the rosary aloud whenever we were working in order to, "elevate our minds to God and help avoid useless chatter," or, as in this case, to keep an aspirant from getting herself into even deeper shit than she was already in by preventing impromptu anatomy lessons.

I pulled out my rosary. "The first sorrowful mystery," I began, aware of the irony of my choice. The first sorrowful mystery, I thought, was not The Agony of Jesus in the Garden, but rather that this thirty-year-old woman did not know where her clit was.

As I started the Apostles' Creed, I realized couldn't see Sister Shanista's right hand anymore.

She had parted her clothing and was clearly groping around trying to locate the topic of conversation. Since we wore no less than four layers between our skin and the outside world, this was not an easy feat.

She was close enough to touch me, and she reached over, grabbed my chin hard and made me look at her.

"Where?" she demanded.

"I don't know, everyone is different. But it's not far from where you pee. It feels different when you touch it than any other place on your body."

And then, without realizing it, I made that two-fingered universal gesture for female masturbation which even if done somewhat hesitantly is a very good communicator of the type of touch one's clit generally needs to provide immediate pleasure. Especially when you're working with a very motivated learner, which apparently I was.

I watched Sister Shanista's face turn pink in surprise and pleasure and I suddenly found myself sitting on the side of the tub because my legs were shaking. I didn't know what else to do, so I resumed praying the rosary.

I was not even through the first decade when Sister Shanista became completely silent, her whole body turned very red and her face took on a very specific countenance. That look was familiar, I realized, because she had the same expression when she took communion.

We made very awkward eye contact for several moments.

"For the love of Jesus," she said, her face still very, very red.

"For the love of Jesus," I agreed.

We resumed cleaning and praying the rosary, and never spoke of it again.

This interaction with Sister Shanista did not technically break the rule of "not touching other sisters, even in jest." It wasn't just physical touching that was forbidden. We were instructed to keep emotionally separate as well.

The term "particular friendship" was used euphemistically to describe actual lesbian relationships, including relationships in which the two parties were known to take a rare moment when we were not busy to *get* busy. However, the term was also used to leverage homophobia in order to discourage nuns from forming personal friendships with other nuns. You didn't need to be having sex in order to be accused of having a "particular friendship." Demonstrating in any way that you preferred the company of one sister over another or had any type of specific connection with another sister was also seen as problematic. Jesus was our spouse and he was jealous of any other relationships we might have.

This made Jesus sound like a creepy green-eyed husband with the potential of devolving into an actual abusive jerk, which is exactly how I was experiencing Him.

Sister Milagro viewed any authentic emotional sharing with abject horror. Especially suspect were expressions of sorrow in public view. The first advice she gave, no matter what you were struggling with, was "don't think about it."

This is a completely useless piece of counsel because if someone could "just not think about it" they wouldn't be thinking about it in the first place. Has this ever worked? In the history of humankind?

CAVEPERSON #1: Why so glum?

CAVEPERSON #2: (frowning) Saber toothed tiger ate my mate.

CAVEPERSON #1: Oh. Well. Just don't think about it.

CAVEPERSON #2: Oh don't think about it. Oh, what a great idea! (Smiling) Thanks, fellow cavedude, me feel better already!

The second bit of advice Sister Milagro would give was "pray about it." It was a lot like "don't think about it" but with a divine guilt factor that demanded, "Don't think about it, let Jesus think about it."

One Sunday night at dinner Sister Milagro told us the story about how one of the professed sisters found out that her whole family had been killed in ethnic cleansing in Rwanda.

"She just cried about it a little that afternoon, asked to go to bed early, and then never mentioned it again. She wasn't sad because she loved and trusted Jesus so much."

Later that night I pulled one of group sisters aside. "In the unlikely event that my entire family is killed in ethnic cleansing and I just cry about it a little that afternoon, ask to go to bed early and never mention it again, can you do me a favor and smother me with a pillow in my sleep?" She nodded, solemnly.

"And you'll promise the same for me?"

It was a strange but reassuring suicide pact and was also one of perhaps only two or three moments of interpersonal intimacy I experienced during my entire convent experience.

Because of my insufficient docility and because I walked like my shoulders were angry, I was held back as an aspirant for 12 months. This is the MC equivalent of flunking pre-school six times. One day the regional superior Sister took me aside to explain.

"The problem with you, Sister Mercy," she said, "is that you have entirely too much self-esteem." This was an accusation I had never heard before that moment.

Or since.

When we entered the convent we were told to pray for a martyr's death because it was the greatest honor Jesus ever bestowed on a Missionary of Charity. I was not too keen on the martyr idea then. However, after getting up at 4:40 every morning and trudging each day through the sustained unpleasantness of this life, I began to do some math.

"I'm twenty-five and the average lifespan of a white American female is probably seventy-two. That means I'm statistically likely to have around forty-seven more years to live. Forty-seven multiplied by 365, carry the three, equals around 1,739 more MC mornings."

My difficulty with praying for a martyr's death was miraculously cured.

After more than a year of MC life, I still missed toilet paper, my knees hurt constantly, and, because I cried so much, I didn't spend nearly as much time praying as I did rinsing out my handkerchief.

But the event that shattered my convent career wasn't anything particularly dramatic, not nearly as dramatic as teaching a nun to masturbate. The day I decided to leave started like most others, with cleaning the women's shelter.

As nuns, we didn't use disposable sanitary products and, because of the stress of our life, I had been having a continual period for almost three months. As we tidied up the top of the dressers that held the women's personal items, I came across something very beautiful. It was a super plus tampon, shining like a precious jewel. I slipped it into my bra, thrilled with my find.

As I cradled it in my hands later, I remembered I hadn't found the tampon. I had stolen it.

I had stolen a tampon from a homeless person.

I could deal with convent life not making me happy, but this was some pretty convincing proof that it wasn't make me holy either.

On August fifteenth, the Feast of the Assumption, I left the convent, walking through the same door I'd walked in over a year earlier. Sister Milagro, who looked genuinely happy for the first time in many months, could scarcely contain her glee as we got on the subway to the Port Authority where she put me on a Greyhound Bus headed for Philadelphia.

I arrived in Philadelphia two-and-half hours later. I felt sorry for the woman sitting next to me, who seemed to speak no English and had to share a seat with a greasy woman with tangled hair wearing the world's most mismatched shirt and skirt combination, alternately sobbing something about being "divorced from Jesus" and praying the rosary out loud. I went to stay with my sister, who generously allowed me time and space to rebuild my life despite the fact she had a two-year-old and a brand new baby.

In the months after I left, I spent a lot of time staring at my feet, looking for work, and using a slide ruler and hand-held calculator to figure out just how long I'd have to spend in purgatory for messing up my engagement to God. Eventually, I found a job, got an apartment, got into therapy, joined a softball team, and went back to school.

I no longer buy into many of the tenets of the Catholic faith as lived by the MCs. Most notably, I no longer believe I suck as a human being. But I miss having a place to hang my spiritual hat. Groovy incense, baby butch nuns, priests in drag, sure this was part of the convent's attraction, but there was a certain reassurance in knowing I had all the answers and if everyone thought just like me then the world would be fine. I suppose in some ways I miss the unambiguous nature of convent thought. It was also nice to the know exactly what was the expected action at any moment, even though it was rare that I could actually live up to the expectation.

I don't have much of a replacement theology. I guess these days I just ask myself if my actions are making the world a better place. I let life be messy and try not to be an asshole.

Am I still in love with the MCs? Yes. Of course.

Now I believe that I deserve more than a spirituality that requires me to repress any part of myself: emotional, intellectual or sexual. And I believe that a phone book is never an acceptable alternative to a roll of toilet paper.

But I do kind of like the Mistress part.

Boi Versus Boy Scout

I once agreed to go whitewater rafting with some friends and fancied myself quite a good sport for being so amenable. Had I known in advance that the weekend we chose for our outing was the same two days that the rafting company was hosting a Boy Scout Jamboree, perhaps I would have reconsidered.

The ubiquitous Boy Scouts posed no particular threat to my fairly traditional-looking lesbian friends, none of whom are ever mistaken for pubescent boys. I, on the other hand, am routinely challenged by the truancy police for being out on the street during school hours even though I am well into my fourth decade of life. As we unloaded our gear, grown men in scoutmaster uniforms, on three separate occasions, asked me where my "buddy" was. However, when I looked perplexed and shrugged, they quickly let the matter drop, so I assumed that would be the end of the confusion.

When we were boarding the buses for the take-off point where we would be putting our rafts into the water, I got herded away from my friends and looked up to find myself surrounded by unfamiliar young male faces. For a moment I thought I might have to pull out a breast or two to convince the scoutmaster to let me off the bus. Instead I just looked pained and said, "I gotta, um, go," which he interpreted as the universal cry of a child to whom nature is calling.

As I made my way back to my friends, it did occur to me that I should add some kind of significant age or gender marker to my outfit that day. A huge pink bow in my hair, or a laminated copy of my driver's license around my neck perhaps. But this was never more than a passing thought, as I was fixated on only two things. First, my goal was to look as cool as possible in my ill-fitting wet suit, and second, I wanted to not fall out of the raft. I should have been more worried about the latter than the former, because after being on the river less than 15 minutes, a large wave hit my side of the raft. My desperate grip and almost-cool look were not enough to keep me from being jettisoned into the water.

Within moments of my splashdown, a scoutmaster had jumped into the water and was swimming to me. Thanks to my life vest, I was bobbing easily in the water and squinting to look for my friends. The scoutmaster, however, had clearly mistaken me for one of his young charges and thought my life was in immediate peril. I don't know if you've ever been saved when you're not actually drowning, but it's a fair amount of work for both people. After a rather protracted rescue, he got me into the raft. What followed was a long awkward silence after he realized he hadn't rescued a drowning Boy Scout, but had annoyed an adult female.

The Boy Scout motto is "Be Prepared" but I have a feeling nothing in his life had prepared Scoutmaster Helpypants for that moment. I spent the next few hours in the boat with the Boy Scouts, more than 100 yards away from my friends. When the Boy Scouts thought I wasn't looking, they snuck glances at each other. One pointed to my chest and mouthed, "Why does he have boobs?"

One particularly brave lad even reached over, tapped my leg and asked, "What troop are you from?"

I answered, "A drag troupe, OK?"

Preoccupied as they were with me, the Boy Scouts were not paying much attention to the commands of the guides and, because of our collective inaction, our small raft flipped no fewer than seven times. Three hours later, as we bailed desperately in hopes of emptying our raft enough to float to our ending point, one of the Boys Scouts wailed, "I wish this was just a video game I was playing."

I nodded and said, "Me too, little man, me too."

Pudding Day

The Conference

In July 2005, I was just another queer performer signed up to entertain at just another queer conference.

When I went to picked up my nametag I printed "kinky poly switch looking for you" under my name in Sharpie. Later that evening my pal Bevin, who was hosting the Friday night entertainment, told the crowd what was on my nametag and then pointed me out from the stage.

"Some queers go to conferences for the politics," she said, "and some go for the sex."

The next day, as I ate a boxed lunch from the Newark Airport Hilton, a beautiful, tall woman dressed in a white skirt covered with orange flowers approached me. She looked me full on for no less than thirty seconds before she spoke and then said simply, "kinky poly switch looking for you? I'm looking for you too."

My dorky response was, "Um, well now I don't know what to say next."

Luckily, she did. "Just meet me after the show tonight."

I didn't even know her name. I asked around about her by describing her features. A friend responded "Oh, whoa, that's Heather Mac. She's gonna kick your ass." I heard a rumor that she peed glitter, which Heather didn't dispel. When I asked her about it later, she only replied, "It gives new meaning to the term 'golden showers' doesn't it?"

I approached her soon after she finished her burlesque numbers that night. "Um can I. Um. Can I um. Help you um carry something?" She smiled the teeniest tiniest smile and we went to her room. She put on a leopard print gown and then we talked. We found we shared the same home state. We found our that we shared bizarrely mixed class backgrounds. We also learned that we both went to Christian high schools and knew all the words to the obscure evangelical chorus "The Trumpet of Jesus." Almost as an afterthought, we negotiated play limits.

The next eight hours are a complete endorphin blur. I cleaned her boots with my tongue. She bit the back of my neck. There was a great deal of poking and then later, even more different types of poking. As she left my room that night-turned-morning, trying to get her to stay I said, "I'd like to see if burlesque queens wake up with glittery lips."

"Maybe someday, if you're lucky, you'll find out," she said, kissing me.

The conference was over the next day and when we said goodbye, she seemed surprised when I asked to stay in touch. I was very horny and completely hooked. What's a cross-country plane ticket when you just had the best sex of your life?

The next day I missed my subway stop twice because I was thinking about the activities of the previous night.

When she called to check in I asked her, "So can I come to California one weekend and be your boi?"

She answered without hesitation, "Hell yeah."

By the time she called me six days later to say, "I dreamed about you last night," I already had my ticket in hand.

The first visit was delightful. The first morning of the first visit I woke up and stared at her. "Wow, I'm exactly where I want to be," I said. She rubbed my head, gave me the most beautiful smile and said, "It's a nice feeling isn't it?"

Shortly before I made the trip, I had heard a rumor that Heather had been diagnosed a few years previously with ovarian cancer. That weekend though, we didn't talk about it. When you're having hot sex, you don't stop to cross-examine someone about cancer. You just have hot sex.

Although I returned home to Philadelphia, we continued to deepen our relationship, talking every morning on the phone. And I set about romancing Heather with great zeal.

I sent flowers.

I sent chocolate.

I sent balloons.

I sent emails.

At some point, I decided I needed to apply some graphic persuasion. I talked a couple of friends into taking progressively more naked pictures of me on a Provincetown beach one August night.

We used the car's headlights to create the perfect mood and got caught by a park ranger. He had apparently been stationed in Provincetown for a long time because his only question was "Is this for commercial use?"

I thought, "Dude have you ever watched porn, ever in your life? Chubby little boi dykes, yes, all the rage in commercial porn."

We had an uncomfortable moment when the park ranger asked for ID. "Someone has to take responsibility for this."

We were silent and looked sheepishly at each other. One friend was a therapist. Another friend was a college teacher. I'm a nurse. None of us wanted to take responsibility for it. We had three licenses to protect. We stalled.

He finally let us off with a sternly worded warning that you can't "take naked pictures on the National Seashore." Even with the interruption, I still had enough photos to send Heather a new one every day for a month.

Goodbye Life, Hello Death

In the meantime, Heather was on tour with her burlesque troupe and her CA-125 was rocketing.

It turns out those cancer rumors I had heard were true. CA-125, short for Cancer Antigen 125, is a protein that is found more in ovarian cancer cells than in other cells. A CA-125 blood test is a good indicator of whether a person with ovarian cancer is responding to treatment. A high score is bad. When I met Heather, she had beaten her CA-125 down to less than twenty-five, which is just below normal. She did it with a combination of surgery, chemo, yoga, long walks, acupuncture, awesome interpersonal support, and orneriness.

By the time she got back from tour it was 997.

It didn't take very long until her growing ovarian tumors started to profoundly affect Heather's everyday health. She was back on chemo and she was vomiting many times each day.

She would call me early in the morning, knowing I was an early riser and would be up in the middle of her San Francisco night. And they were long nights. She'd often start with, "I've got 45 minutes until I can take more Dilaudid. Can you talk me through it?"

I resisted the urge to say, "Um no, I don't think I can. I think I am unqualified to talk you through such a situation." So, I tried. I read to her sometimes, mostly David Sedaris. I told her knock-knock jokes my niece and nephew had passed along to me. I related road tales from my stand-up comedy travels. And after weeks and weeks of feeling worse and worse, more and more often, she started to say things like, "How much fighting is enough?"

I never knew the right answer to that. I tried every random assortment of words assembled in the English language. She was a bit of a cancer expert by this time, and she gave me some coaching. "Boi when things are this bad there are only two things you can say. 'I'm sorry' and 'that sucks.'"

The next day I went to church despite an absence of many years. I wore my "Jesus is coming, hide the porn" t-shirt underneath my hoodie. I felt as if I was drowning in helplessness, and the familiar liturgy soothed me.

We'd been dating six months at this point but Heather didn't want me to visit. She thought it would sully our new relationship for me to see her so ill. Still, I pestered her. I was visiting a friend in Portland when she called me.

"How come you're visiting everyone on the West coast but me?"

"You've got to be fucking kidding me," I said, and drove down the next day.

She was as beautiful as ever but looked much sicker than I had imagined. She was consuming almost nothing by this point, but she would sit in the bed with me at 4 a.m., eating very small bits of ice cream off the shared spoon. Her mouth was white with a fungal infection but I never got it, despite our nocturnal spit swapping.

From a combination of meds and an infection, Heather became more and more confused. One night I awoke to find her sitting cross legged and fully awake, watching me. She spoke as soon as I opened my eyes. "I was going to finish your circumcision. But I couldn't find the scissors." Fortunately she wasn't too insistent, and I was exhausted so I fell back asleep. Just to be safe, the next morning I hid everything sharp in the room.

Even when she didn't exactly make cognitive sense, she was still there. One early morning I was awakened by her efforts to peel off my shirt. She was sleeping topless too.

"I just wanted to feel," she explained, "your skin on my skin."

Later that week, I called her from the grocery store and asked if I could bring her anything. She had been nauseous for six weeks. She spat back, "Pick me up a quarter pound of the will to live." I said "Oh, I'm at Trader Joe's and you know how they are. They only had organic and now they're all out."

She immediately replied, "Damn, I had a coupon, too."

A little more than a week into my visit, was the day that I came to think of as Evil Tuesday. Heather's socially awkward oncologist gave her the news that her body's cells were too damaged by chemo to have more chemo. He also said that Heather had only a few weeks to live and recommended that she find a nice hospice in which to die.

The hospital's kick-ass oncology social worker heard about the situation and met with us to help with the hospice search. Since Heather had an ever-evolving entourage of friends, lovers and ex-lovers, she asked her usual question, "And who do you have here to support you today?"

Heather introduced Karen, the partner of one of her oldest friends who was visiting from Portland and then looked at me. "How to explain Kelli," she shrugged. "Kelli is my boi."

The social worker nodded and continued on with her questions.

Later that day when the social worker wanted to ask me a question, she sought permission from Heather before she approached me. It was as if she had a sensitivity training from Kinky Leatherpeople of America that morning. It was typical San Francisco. There was probably a box on the patient intake form that read, "Do you have a full time submissive? Check yes or no."

The first hospice we went to visit was a barely converted convent. As we sat in what had been the nuns' reception parlor, Heather, remembering that my days in the convent were not smooth, asked sweetly, "Is this giving you flashbacks or anything?"

I wanted to say, "This a not a day to have flashbacks, this seems more like a day to cause flashbacks." Instead, I was just silent, while she held my pinkie in her hand. She scratched my palm a little bit and said, "You know if this is where I die, I'm going to make sure I fuck you 'til you bleed on the floor first." She looked sideways at me.

"Well then," I said, wondering a little if the staff had overheard.

It was a strange day.

When we got back to the hospital's cancer resource center, we talked through options. I heard Heather say, "Oh, hi Annie," and I turned around and standing there, like some kind of sex positive queer cavalry, stood Annie Sprinkle.

Although it made sense that she and Heather knew each other, her appearance from seemingly out of nowhere was surreal. She sat with Heather, searching for resources, talking and generally being an encouraging and soothing presence.

That night when we returned home and were lying in bed, I kissed Heather on her forehead. I was perplexed. It didn't even make sense. How could someone be so present, so *here* how could the warm skin that I was touching be cold in just a few weeks? Heather asked me what I was thinking.

I responded with a non committal *i-dunno* sound.

To my great surprise, just then she reached over and grabbed my tits.

And it was on.

And I never answered the question, because when you're having hot sex, you don't stop to talk about death. You just have hot sex.

Goodbye Death, Hello Life

The next day I had to go back to Philadelphia for a week because I had already missed a lot of work and didn't want to lose the job too. I was called out of a 2 p.m. meeting by one of Heather's friends who was in a state of what sounded very much like panic.

"Where is Heather?"

I was silent for a moment, confused by the question.

"What do you mean, where's Heather? I'm in Philadelphia. I don't know. I didn't kidnap her."

Heather, who had been given two weeks to live by the socially awkward oncologist who refused to give her anymore chemo on the grounds that it might kill her?

Heather, who seemed to not be aware of what day of the week it was? And was seldom even getting out of bed?

She was missing.

That morning as I was getting into the taxi to go the airport, Heather had called her friend V and invited her for a visit. V called herself a "cancer vixen, not victim." V had been given a terminal diagnosis almost a decade before.

While she waiting for V, Heather called her scheduled afternoon visitor and said she had some other help lined up. When V came to the door, Heather was sitting in the living room with a bag packed.

She instructed V, "Take me to your oncologist."

And because people usually did what Heather told them to, V took Heather to her oncologist, who was 70 miles away in Santa Cruz. V's oncologist looked at Heather, called for her medical records and decided if Heather was willing to try another form of chemo, she was willing to give it her. Heather responded to this chemo and immediately began to get better.

It's not just anyone who, when they're so close to the Grim Reaper that they can smell his nasty breath, will decide to pack a bag, run away from home, and save their own life. But Heather MacAllister was not just anyone.

Hail Mary, What A Place

Two weeks later Heather called me and her voice sounded so strong I almost didn't recognize her. "So boi, are we still up for that pilgrimage to Lourdes? You gonna score me that miracle cure?"

Lourdes, France is a holy place for Catholics because, in the mid-nineteenth century, an apparition of the Virgin Mary was reported on fourteen separate occasions by a teenage girl named Bernadette Soubirous. After a number of alleged miracles occurred there, it has become a pilgrimage spot for millions of devout Catholic pilgrims. Millions of devout Catholic pilgrims, that is, and us.

It's not that Heather and I were practicing Catholics exactly, although we called ourselves ironic Catholics in a completely unironic way. You take a miracle cure where you can get it.

We made plans to go. We didn't make plans for what we would do once we got there. We were skipping museums and monuments in barter for a miracle. Since the usual miracle-seeking path involved a dip in the sacred pools that have collected from the spring that Bernadette discovered, that was our only agenda item for our stay.

Once in the village of Lourdes, I accompanied Heather to the building where volunteers helped pilgrims lower themselves into the sixty-degree pools. I waited awkwardly for a moment, stuck for something to say.

"Good. Uh. Luck." But she was already in the door.

I waited outside, reclining on the warm lawn and playing a game of Spot the Nun. After what seemed like a very long while I felt a few drops of water on my face and turned. The spray was coming from Heather, towering over me and shaking. She had obviously had quite a cry. This did not seem like a positive sign.

She spat, "Jesus Christ, they didn't even have any towels!"

I countered with a tentative, "So, um, how do you...feel?"

"The same," she said, and then after a moment added, "but colder. Much fucking colder."

"I'm sorry," I said, getting up.

She took my hand "Yup, it sucks."

We walked back towards the hotel where we were staying and Heather sent me to get some food. Not an easy task as Heather was eating a vegan diet, and we were in rural France. I returned to the hotel two hours later with the only non-meat, non-cheese item I could find: a medium sized bag of salt and vinegar potato chips.

She didn't mind though. "Just. Whatever. I'm hungry. Set the table and we'll eat."

Ten minutes later, she was glaring at me across the table laden with potato chips. We both reached for the bag and then started giggling.

"So far, this trip sucks!" I said almost unable to get the words out in between laughs.

"It sucks ass."

The next morning we got a train from Lourdes to head over to another small town in the south of France, where many of Heather's friends were staying together in a borrowed house. I went to check on our luggage after Heather was safely aboard. Unfortunately I didn't note the track number and so once I had completed my errand there was a frantic ten minutes of searching for the right train. If

Heather hadn't leaned out the open door and waved to me, I might be still standing on that platform.

An American tourist, who was seated across from us and had been watching our little comedy, said in an exaggerated California surfer boy accent, "Dude, it's a frickin' miracle you all found one another."

Heather ruffled my newly sweaty hair.

She said, "Yeah, that is our frickin' miracle," and kissed my cheek as I sat down.

Asking

While Heather was fighting for her life, in some ways I was fighting to be a part of her life. I had been asking Heather all along if I could come to the West coast and be with her. My style of romancing Heather was based on a strategy of repetition and subsequent wear down.

Now, both of us cuddled on a twin bed in a bright white bedroom on the second floor of the borrowed house in the South of France while her friends played a French card game downstairs. I asked again and finally she acquiesced. She lay next to me on her bed, playing with my pinkie finger.

"But before you come out I need you to understand, I don't know how long I have. If it gets to the point where the pain or the nausea is too bad, I'm going to take my own life. I need to know the people closest to me aren't going to oppose me."

I wasn't surprised. She had mentioned hastening her own death before. I nodded, and she kissed the tear that was running down my cheek.

And then we had sex and didn't talk about it anymore. When you're having hot sex, you don't stop to talk about assisted suicide. You just have hot sex.

Someone asked me if it was hard to decide to move to be with Heather. Deciding wasn't hard at all. Someone you really love almost died, and then didn't, and runs away and saves her own life and might live for a while longer and might not. And they live 3000 miles away. And they have logistical needs than can be partially met by someone with your skillset and mindset and also heartset. What other possible choice is there?

It wasn't a hard choice, it was a joyous one. Actually living out that decision was difficult, but making the decision was a simple "hell yeah."

I went home to give notice at my day job, and one rainy Wednesday afternoon Heather called me.

"Hey boi," she said, tentatively. That was a tone I almost never heard in her voice.

"I've got a big favor to ask you." She didn't even stop to take a breath. "Instead of you moving to San Francisco, how about we move to Portland."

I, on the other hand, took a very big breath. "Wow, move to Portland, home of the hippies and no stand-up comedy? That is a big favor."

I sat while she explained. Heather loved the Bay Area, but she was poor and sick, and San Francisco is an especially hard place to be both. Her disability check would go a lot further in Oregon, and she had a lot of old friends and lovers in Portland who wanted to be more directly supportive.

I wasn't too keen on moving to Portland, but Heather seemed very sure and so I followed along.

We moved into a place together, a partly converted Hare Krisha Temple in one of Portland's northeast neighborhoods.

The place was ideal, in many ways, for us. The main area upstairs was over 700 square feet and we decided it was large enough to put on a show and have an audience, perfect for two performers living under one roof. The downstairs had a kitchen, two more rooms which we made into my room, and a guest room, and all sorts of wacky features, including not one but two sets of concrete stairs that went nowhere. The back yard included a beautiful garden with a mature grape arbor, a teeny tiny pond and a statue of the Virgin Mary. The space that Heather picked out for her bed was on the raised platform in the front of the big room.

Heather's bed was on a stage. Strange. Perfect.

We started referring to our place as The Castle, partly because of its size, and partly because I had taken to calling Heather my Queen. She had adopted the moniker "Chevalier" for me, a term we appropriated from the French and which means approximately "chief knight" although in my case, Heather said, it actually meant "chief dork." The idea behind labeling our relationship was thus: Heather was the Queen, engaged in a fight for her life with cancer. As the head knight, I would take care of all the details of life around the castle, so that she could concentrate on her own scary and important battle.

It sounds a bit portentous looking back on it, but mostly it meant I did the laundry and made a lot of smoothies.

Getting Along

There's a time in every newly co-habitating couple's life when one looks at the other and asks, "Seriously though. Seriously. Were you raised by wolves?"

I was scattered. I lost Heather's $200 prescription sunglasses. I was overconfident in my abilities, insisting that I could make a bathtub from used building materials. Most of all, I was grossly solicitous.

Heather had pretty effective ways of communicating that she did not want me quite so far up her ass. For example, one day when she was getting chemo at the outpatient clinic

I fussed around, getting her graham crackers and tea she didn't ask for. Finally, when she fell asleep, I rubbed her hand and said in what I thought was a soothing voice, "It's okay, I'm right here, you're doing great."

Heather opened one eye and said, "Who the fuck are you, the chemo whisperer?"

When she changed pain medications, dosages were confused and she had taken what I thought to be a dangerously high amount. She seemed very sedated, so I slept on the couch and tiptoed in to check on her frequently. She thought it was too frequently, and, at one point as soon as I entered, I saw that her eyes were wide open and her chest was not moving. I ran to the bed, started to shake her and said "my Queen, my Queen!" Just then she grabbed me by the shoulders and said "gotcha!"

It took me probably five minutes to catch my breath, and she was overcome with giggles the entire time, taken with her own cleverness.

I stared her down. "That's never going to happen again, right?"

She corrected: "That's never going to happen again, right, Ma'am?" Beat. She goaded, "So now there can only be one comic in the family?"

She didn't apologize or even really stop laughing, but she also never faked her death again. I had been worried about safety, but to Heather, dignity was much more important.

Fluid Bonding

Neither one of us were any kind of prize going into the relationship. We both had issues around trust and letting each other in. A lot of our intimacy those first few months of living together came in the form of fluid bonding. Not fluid bonding as in the harm reduction strategy for decreasing rate of STI transmissions. No, when you're really sick, you have to deal with body fluids not always being where you expect them to be. We bonded a lot around that.

One night Heather could not stop throwing up, and we ended up at the ER. We arrived to a very full waiting room. As Heather approached the triage station where a nurse sat surrounded by the walls of her see through cubicle, Heather bent over a bit to speak into the microphone. Then she projectile vomited against the Plexiglas wall. We watched the vomit drip down the glass.

Heather was not too sick to be completely mortified. I stood beside her in silence for a moment and then had an idea.

Because I have had multiple stomach surgeries, I sometimes have some surprising GI problems myself. I turned to Heather and said, "Would this be a good moment to tell you about the time I shit on the walls of my therapist's bathroom?"

She almost smiled, visibly cheered. "I actually feel better already."

Another late night when Heather was on medication that made her pee constantly, I woke up to her exasperated plea, "C'mon, boi, get up we gotta change the sheets, I pissed the bed." Exhausted, I shook my head, "Can we just change sides? I'll sleep just as well in a puddle of your pee as I will on dry sheets."

She reluctantly acquiesced and we both fell quickly back to sleep. We both woke up the next morning horny as hell. We fucked until five minutes before she needed to leave for chemo. Heather insisted I could skip my shower since we had so little time.

I responded, "Um, actually I don't think I can skip my shower. I'm covered in your pee."

She nodded. "Yeah maybe better to be late in this case."

We had the infusion center to ourselves that morning and we laughed about our earlier adventures. Heather bopped me on the head with the book she had been reading, "Well if I can pee the bed, and you can like sleeping in it, and I can like you sleeping in it. Well, I guess we're going to make it just fine."

I put my hand on her leg and repeated "Yup, just fine"

It amazed me that Heather would start a brand new relationship, one that she told a friend during our first month living together made her "feel giggly like a teenager," at a point when most people might be doing the emotional equivalent of curling up on the couch and eating Oreos. I guess it's not bad to have an infusion of relatively new relationship energy when you are really sick. The other person doesn't get as tired of fetching you things. Or making you smoothies, even though you can never drink them.

Some of our time those early months were taken up with cancer business: chemo, insurance, dealing with side effects from chemo, negotiating the complications when treatment wasn't working. But we had a lot of fun too. We went on short hikes to Oregon's historic hot springs, we went through the hay bale maze at the Portland Fir Farm which, as it turned out, was in the heterosexual part of Oregon. We bought important fall supplies, including a whole heap of pumpkins for our Halloween Party. We proved that you can, with some effort, fit three average hay bales in a Toyota Camry.

We had seventy-five people at the Castle for a Halloween party. Heather got out of bed to host, wearing her regal blue-green floor length gown she had bought at the San Francisco Opera used costume sale a few years before. She hosted a surprise costume contest. It was a surprise to me anyway. We had never discussed having such a contest and she gave away some of our random household items as prizes.

We were having fun, but as the year drew to a close, the chemo stopped working and cancer became less of a background matter and more the focus of our daily lives.

The day after Thanksgiving, Heather made two decisions. First, since it was only making her sick and was not beating back her cancer much she was going to go off chemo. Second, we were going to have a great Christmas. I was saddened and a little bit surprised by her pronouncement. I wasn't expecting her to stop chemo so soon. It was not my choice to make though, so I dedicated my efforts to the decision to have a good Christmas. I turned the Castle inside out with an approximation of holiday cheer.

The next weekend Heather's sisters and grandma came to visit and we got a tree, a really big tree, that even in our cavernous space, loomed large. We had all our homo friends over to string cranberries and popcorn to trim it.

Heather personalized a stocking for me by writing "Boi" in glitter on its cuff. "Chevalier," she explained, had way too many letters. She already had her own stocking, complete with leopard print piping. We didn't have a chimney, so we hung our stockings by a large mirror with care.

I personally couldn't imagine Santa including creature-loving Portland in his flight plan; he would surely get slapped with some kind of cruelty to animals citation for making the reindeer fly so far in one night. I wondered out loud if there was a special hippie Santa just for Portland. A gender non-specific person who would probably bike in, wearing hemp shoes and a Guatemalan vest. Heather told me to shut up and stop being a cynic, but still laughed really hard when I left hummus and soymilk by our makeshift chimney, just in case.

Christmas morning, after we had opened our gifts and before I headed downstairs to begin cooking dinner for the gang we would be having over in the afternoon, Heather took my hand. She was silent for a long moment and then said, "You know, most people would think I'm unlucky because I'll be dead before I turn 40. But, I actually think I am quite lucky. There are so few people in the world who have been loved by someone the way I have been loved by you."

Heather had great support in Portland and so I did too. But while I knew I didn't have the option of completely falling apart, I could feel pieces of me breaking off in the brittleness of thinking of life without her.

We were at her favorite Whole Foods when she left for another aisle without telling me. When she returned I was crying.

"I couldn't find you," I explained in response to her expression of consternation.

She made silent eye contact for a long moment.

"Were you thinking that one day you'll come here and you really won't be able to find me?"

I nodded, quietly sobbing now.

She thought.

"When I'm dead you won't be at the natural foods store buying organic produce. You'll be back at Safeway picking up $1.99 hot dogs."

She took my hand and we finished shopping.

Snowballs and Snoopy

We started with home hospice after the New Year. The hospice nurses made everything easier, but I think we confused them a little bit. On the afternoon they were coming to do intake, there had been a rare Portland snow and it was very wet. It was the kind of sticky white stuff that makes perfect snowballs.

Heather was outside smoking, I was attempting to shovel the sidewalk in front of our house with a broom. When I walked past our car, I scooped up a handful of snow.

Heather said, "I know you aren't about to start a snowball fight, boi."

I countered with a question. "Um, am I?"

I was thinking furiously because I couldn't figure out if it was an awesome idea or a horrible one. I lobbed a test snowball in her general direction.

She responded by grabbing two huge handfuls of snow and putting them down the neck of my thermal, and when I tried to run away she pelted me with more snow, hastily grabbed from the roof of our car.

I ran across the street and threw snowballs at her from behind the safety of a neighbor's SUV.

Just then the hospice nurse drove up. We both adopted a very innocent demeanor. It is entirely possible that I whistled.

The hospice nurse said "Are you all...were you...I mean... was this? Are you guys having a snowball fight?"

Heather sniffed. "A person's got a little stage four ovarian cancer and all of sudden she's not supposed to be having snowball fights? What's it gonna do, kill me?"

The hospice nurse nodded and said "That is a very good point."

We all went inside and I took a moment to go downstairs and collect myself. Heather and I couldn't look at each other for the rest of the visit without breaking into giggles.

We confused the hospice folks a fair amount.

One of the most effective tension breakers in our house was me, doing the Snoopy Dance. It started originally as part of my stand-up act. Because I went to a fundamentalist Christian high school that labeled dancing as "the devil's work," I never learned how to dance socially, and so everything I knew about dancing I learned from watching the kids in *Peanuts*. Arms straight out, hopping off alternating feet, head turning from side to side.

I started doing it for Heather when she needed cheering up and somehow it became a strip tease. Not really an erotic dance, but I did take off all my clothes. When Heather's sisters were visiting, she asked me to do the Snoopy Dance for them and I reminded her that it was a strip tease number. She shrugged. "You're a comic, improvise."

So I did the Snoopy Dance for Heather's sisters, incorporating various props from around the living room and not taking off any of my clothes. I was running out of moves when I hit upon around the idea of inserting a random scene from *Cats* halfway through. Since I've never seen *Cats*, I simply improvised, making cat pawing motions and then, spying a Sharpie on the living room table, drew cat whiskers on my face.

Once the Snoopy Dance was over, Heather went upstairs to take a nap. Somehow the conversation with her sisters turned to the subject of microwaving peeps. They had never seen the carnage that results when a peep is microwaved, which seemed impossible and even a bit sad to me, so I showed them. We became quite taken with the idea of microwaving various sugary treats and since it was just after Christmas the house was full of them. Soon we had a paper plate full of Jujubes, a sour apple Now and Later, cherry jelly slices, and red hots in various states of melting.

Forty minutes later as I was cleaning up the mess from our kitchen science experiments, I heard a knock on the door. Forgetting both the cat whiskers I had drawn on my face, and the fact that I held a painting pallet of melted junk food, I answered.

It was the hospice nurse.

Heather had started on a central IV pump for pain medications that week, so I sat down with the nurse to go over some of the details of flushing the pump, checking the tubes for patency, and administering meds. If she thought it strange to have a discussion with another nurse about the nursing procedures for end of life care with someone who had cat whiskers drawn on their face with a marker, she gave no outward indication.

Although I can't help thinking she went back to the her office and said, "those queers, they're sweet, but when they're sad, they have some *awfully* interesting grief and caregiving rituals."

The Decision

The next few weeks grew steadily more difficult for Heather. She had unremitting pain that continued even when we were giving her intravenous pain medication around the clock. She had also been essentially unable to eat and many nights we were up until sunrise, sometimes with hospice present, trying to get her symptoms under control.

Physician assisted suicide is legal in Oregon and Heather had already begun the paperwork to obtain the meds to help her hasten her death if she got to that point. One night in early February, I was sleeping curled up beside her when I heard her talking on the phone.

"Yeah, you better get here as quick as you can. I've had enough. I'm doing it tomorrow." I waited until she finished the phone call and then poked her with the very tip of my pinkie.

"Hey, my Queen," I said, continuing to poke her lightly, "when a person decides they are going to use assisted suicide to hasten their death, they're supposed to tell the person sleeping beside them *before* they start telling the world."

"Ooooh that's right," she said, almost mocking me, "I'm sorry. I forgot that was the procedure." And then kissed me, open mouthed, for a moment. And then we didn't say anything more. Because when you're in the middle of a hot kiss, you don't stop to talk about the fact that in a few short hours the person you're kissing will be gone from you forever. You just enjoy the hot kiss.

We looked at each other for a moment and then I got out of bed, put on some water for tea, and started helping Heather make her phone calls.

By that Tuesday at 7:30 a.m. everything was in place. The assisted suicide liaison, Barbara Gideon, perhaps the straightest person I have ever seen, was sitting on our couch surrounded by forms.

She made conversation with our gathered tribe as she sifted through the paperwork, sitting primly with her legs crossed in her Ann Taylor suit. She looked as if this was all very customary and in that, this was the fourth house of freaks she had been to today.

Also on the couch was Blaze, Heather's long time lover, with whom she had a Daddy/girl relationship at one time that had morphed into a lovely comfortable sexual/romantic friendship. Blaze, with her full beard, furry body and almost bearlike grumpiness was practically a caricature of herself. She also loved Heather with her entire being and made her laugh, especially when no one else could.

Heather's two best friends were making coffee in the kitchen. Sandy, the quintessential child of hippies, covered in tattoos and wearing thigh leather boots for the occasion, lived in Portland. When things were particularly hard or we got really bad news, she would show up with her signature popcorn, flavored with nutritional yeast and goddess knows what else. Tatiania, Heather's friend since their shared Michigan days, had been flying up nearly every weekend from San Francisco. She had just gotten home when we had called her to come back.

Heather's biological sisters were bleary-eyed. One almost asleep on Heather's bed and the other slumped in our giant easy chair. They had flown in from the Midwest the night before. Hannah, the middle sibling, was a federal agent. Initially, we were all a little nervous around her, especially the potheads, but somehow both she and Heidi managed to fit right in. We were all very much acting like a family.

Hannah had brought her husband Edward, a blonde, blue-eyed buzzcut straight dude who was a traffic cop. At one point, he went outside to make a phone call and Hannah heard him whispering in almost reverential tone. "Yeah and there are ma'ams and bois and boi is spelled with an *i* and she's a girl!"

About halfway through the day, someone handed Edward a five-year-old Sports Illustrated stolen from the tattoo shop down the street. He gamely paged through it, acting as if the scores of the college games that happened nearly a half dozen years ago fascinated him.

Standing against the wall in our large living room was someone I called Woo Woo Cindi. Cindi was present courtesy of the local cancer resource center that had been providing acupuncture and massage services free for Heather for almost a year. She was a 70's lesbian who talked a lot about trees, energy work, organic kale, being grounded, and other things I hate. She had been present at a lot of people's "transitions."

There were other folks too. The Radical Faeries stopped in and out, bringing with them the smell of both patchouli and body odor as well as their sweetness and as much Reiki as anyone in the house wanted.

Our friend Stephanie had been at The Castle for a few days running. She was in charge of supplying Heather's online support group, the Lovetroopers, with up to the minute communications and with making me laugh.

As our new pal Barbara Gideon waded through the forms, we all alternately kept it together and lost it. The potheads smoked a lot of pot. I drank my own weight in Diet Mountain Dew. At some point, we ate Popeye's chicken. Heather drank a Pepsi, cuddled with each of us in turn, and when she was craving a cigarette and was headed outside to the porch, stopped and thought for a moment.

"Wait, I don't smoke inside because I don't want to get my clothes and stuff smelly. I'm not going to have to worry about that anymore."

She smoked her last cigarette sitting on the couch.

The End

There's surprisingly little to say about our goodbyes. If it hasn't been said up to that point, it's not going to get worked out while the person is waving back over their shoulder at you. Once Heather took time to express her love to each of us and gave out appropriate bits of advice in turn, she was, in a very real way, already gone. She was simply, as she said it, "tired and done." And as the moment got closer, she seemed almost delighted in her final act of self-determination after so many months of intractable pain and nausea as well as being held captive to the whims and torments of the health care system.

In fact, that morning when she woke up she looked at me and said "Oh, you're still here."

I said "thanks a lot" and she laid back with her hands laced behind her head.

"Oh, honey, it's nothing personal It just means I'm not dead yet."

For our goodbyes, I sang my goofy little "who's the best ma'am in this land" song, because that's what I did for her, and she patted me on the head, because that's what she did for me. And then kissed me, open mouthed, and we didn't say anything. Because when you're in the middle of a passionate kiss, you don't stop to talk about how the person you're kissing is going to be lost to you forever in a few minutes. You just enjoy the kiss.

At Heather's request, I gave her the IV anti-nausea drugs that she would need to keep down the assisted suicide meds. As I drew up the dose, I was singing her the Snoopy song but my voice was shaking. I looked into her peaceful face and realized I wasn't trying to cheer up Heather, I was trying to maintain my own courage.

Death On My Pillow

Sandy's partner, Karen, had bravely offered to mix up the lethal dose of medication that Heather had been prescribed. She swirled the white powder into Heather's requested medium, Cozy Shack chocolate pudding.

Karen took the bowl into Heather.

Heather ate the pudding.

She died.

It sucked.

It sucked, but it theoretically sucked less than watching her suffer. We called the hospice nurse who officially declared the death and filled out more paperwork and then I made the call to the funeral director to come pick up Heather's body.

Stephanie stopped them from taking her body out in a black bag. She insisted on wrapping Heather's body in one of her own leopard print sheets.

And when they finally took her body away, I realized that Heather, of all things, had died not on her own pillow, but on mine.

I was furious.

"Talk about bad organization. This was a planned death. Planned in almost every detail. Isn't there some rule, that if you're going to die, and it's organized and everything, you should have the courtesy to leave other people's bedding out of it?"

It was pretty silent for a minute. Woo Woo Cindi opened her mouth, I'm sure in preparation to talk some shit about how beautiful it was that Heather's energy had transitioned on my pillow. Hannah gave her a very dirty look and she snapped her mouth closed. Perhaps she knew that federal agents always travel armed.

Then Sandy reached forward and hugged me for a really long time and offered me some popcorn. And no one said anything.

The next afternoon I was called out of the shower by Blaze, who grumbled into the bathroom with a Kmart bag which she left on the floor. She shrugged "I, um, brought you something." And then shuffled out.

While I was toweling off, I peeked inside the bag. It contained a brand new pillow.

In a brand new Snoopy pillowcase.

Sister Mercy and The Terrible Horrible No Good Very Bad I'm Probably Going to Go To Hell Day

We're supposed to go to sleep thinking about Jesus but I went to sleep worrying about the tear in my habit and when I got out of bed this morning the sheet we're supposed to dress under got mixed up with the sheet I am supposed to put on and on my way to the chapel I got it caught on the Infant of Prague statue and it tore even a bigger hole and I could tell it was going to be a terrible horrible no good very bad I'm probably going to hell day.

At morning prayer Sister Anna Maria saw angels and Sister Lisa had Jesus talk directly to her but all that happened to me at morning prayer is my knees got just a little more sore.

I think I'll become a lesbian.

At Mass, Sister Milagro let Sister Anna Maria have a seat near the chapel window. Sister Milagro let Sister Lisa have a seat by the chapel window too. I wanted to say I was being scrunched. I wanted to say was being smooshed. I wanted to say if I don't get a seat by the window I am going to be get sick right after I take communion and maybe even throw up the body of Christ. Jesus didn't even answer.

I could tell it was going to be a terrible horrible no good very bad I bet I am probably going to go to hell day.

On our way to work at the soup kitchen, Sister Angeles said that Sister Marie Amabella was more recollected than I was. When it was singing time she said I sang too loud. When I led the rosary, she said I left out the sorrowful mysteries. Who needs the sorrowful mysteries? I could it was going to be a terrible horrible no good very bad I am probably going to go to hell day.

On the way to adoration, Sister Milagro told me I was in charge of setting up holy hour. I was supposed to light the incense from the sanctuary candle and instead I put out the sanctuary candle. When I went to get more matches to light the sanctuary candle again, Sister Milagro came back into the chapel and said I must not love Jesus very much or I wouldn't have left him so lonely with no light burning for people to know he was in the Blessed Sacrament.

I am having a terrible horrible no good very bad day, I whispered to Jesus in the Blessed Sacrament. Jesus didn't even answer.

There were lima beans for dinner and I hate limas. There was no kissing between nuns and I wanted some kissing.

When I went to bed I couldn't find my crucifix or my prayer book or my soap or my underwear. Sister Anna Maria wants to be married to Jesus instead of sleeping with me.

It was a terrible horrible no good very bad I'm probably going to hell day.

My mistress says some days are like that. Even when you're a lesbian.

Performing By the Numbers

Why I Decided To Do Alternative Comedy and How It's Working For Me So Far

Perhaps it's a bit disingenuous to say that I decided to do alternative comedy. It's not as if I sat down at my computer with a spreadsheet and conducted a benefits and risks assessments analysis, using all the copious amounts of objective data about the differing types of comedy performance circuits based on the latest figures from Goldman Sachs.

I was attempting to make it in the world of mainstream comedy clubs with extremely limited success. One night I was trying out new material at the Comedy Cabaret, a disgusting club in Northeast Philadelphia. The men (it was almost all men) who frequented the open mic were The Angry Hobbyist: a species of comics who are not really interested in getting their own HBO special as much as having an excuse to drink copious amounts of alcohol on weeknights and yell horrible things about their ex-wives with some kind of social sanction.

Rape was the airline food of this particular open mic. It was the default subject of comfort, with seemingly endless comic possibilities. One particular fratty-dude would get up every week and the rest of the guys would goad him into telling this particular gem: "I took this girl parking and she said 'hey I'm not that kind of girl' so I took out my knife and said 'yes you are.'"

In the beautiful world of the Comedy Cabaret the rape joke without a punchline was the Holy Grail, the most sought after of all comedic accomplishments. It was always a very comfortable situation for me, my best friend Maura who had seemingly bottomless tolerance for accompanying me to such venues, and whatever other dyke about town we could drag along with us.

One night, I started my set with, "I need you to do me a little favor and ignore every visual cue you're getting right now and believe I am an adult female and not a 12 year old boy." One of the angry hobbyists yelled from the audience "You're not a 12 year old boy. You're just a big fat ugly dyke."

I had one of those comedy moments wherein my lizard brain reacted and didn't even check in with my frontal lobe before it tumbled the words out of my mouth.

"Aw," I said in my most condescending voice, "you're just sad I'm not a 12 year-old boy. You and the Catholic priests both."

Later, Mr. Angry Hobbyist acted in a manner consistent with his name and chased me through the parking lot with a broken bottle. As I hid behind Maura's van, panting, I realized I needed to either become much faster at running or find some more suitable venues.

I still had one more club gig lined up with Dolly, Philadelphia's Queen of Bringer Shows. Dolly was kind of an unusual figure in Philadelphia, not only because she was a female producer in a men's world, but also because she insisted she was missing a hand. She wore a cotton glove and call it her prosthesis and refer to herself as "handicapped" or "handicapable." Yet, when she removed the cotton glove from her "prosthesis," which she did when she was taking a twenty dollar bill from one of the fifteen people you were required to bring to get ten minutes of stage time at one of her shows, it was just a hand. A real hand, not a fake one.

The guy who performed before me at that last show brought a small army of friends so Dolly gave him twenty minutes of stage time. He used that stage time in an attempt to break the world's record for the number of synonyms for "smelly" to be used in the description of a human vagina. He would have made it too, except for he was simultaneously trying to break the record for the number of times a white guy says the n word in a twenty minute stand up set. The folks who came to see this charming fellow thought all of this was absolutely hilarious.

I started my set by sniffing my way up my arm and saying "delicious."

As soon as the show was over I informed Dolly I couldn't perform with a white person who says the n word. She told me that I wasn't far enough along in my career to make those kind of demands. I said I was and that I didn't have sufficient resources to start a separate racist mailing list for folks I could invite to her shows.

Just then we heard a melee from the parking lot. As if to illustrate my point on cue, a brawl had broken out between Mr Racist Van Fish-hater's fans and mine. It took security guards and both of Dolly's hands to break it up.

This is what led me to the alternative comedy scene (still comedy in clubs, just not comedy clubs) and then to the alternative alternative scene which is like off-off-off Broadway, so far off Broadway it's on the moon or at a diner in Cleveland. I started modeling my career after my friends who are indie musicians, building a mailing list, touring and putting out a CD every few years.

For a time, I approached anyone who was assembling any group of people large or small who would be sitting still for any queer or kinky or poly or progressive reason. "This event would be better with comedy," I'd suggest. I became Kelli "I'll emcee that" Dunham. Then, the real fun began.

11 o'clock

11 p.m. is the time the evening entertainment begins at the Rainbow Mountain Resort in Pennsylvania's Poconos Mountains. Since most attendees are staying at the resort and not worried about driving and because they've had all evening to imbibe, the average attention span of an audience member is 2.7 seconds.

I once had an audience member heckle me at Rainbow Mountain Resort after I was introduced but before I was able to reach the stage. No conventional heckler, she yelled, "Your therapist wants to kill herself." I had to provide some spontaneous heckle coaching from stage.

"Um, that's actually not a great heckle, friend. You might try something like 'you suck' or 'you're not funny' or 'get off the stage, boo!' Not 'your therapist wants to kill herself.'"

Only a lesbian would think a good heckle would involve maligning your mental health care. What next? "And your psychiatrist thinks you should be on Paxil but you should really be on an atypical SSRI."

13 Shades of Red

At Rhode Island Pride they gave out little grab bags of gifts from the sponsors. In my bag was a small bottle of clear fluid which I assumed, from its appearance, to be hand sanitizer. So, I was in the Port a John doing what one does in a Port a John and when I came out, quickly squeezed some "hand sanitizer" on my hands before being introduced to the Mayor of Providence. As I pulled my hand away from our handshake, I realized my hand had been extremely sticky, and when I looked at the bottle in my other hand, I saw that it was actually lube.

Now if they had a sexually repressed straight guy as mayor I imagine he could have imagined that I had just eaten some raspberries or handful of any kind of candy that might melt in one's hand rather than one's mouth. But it turns out their mayor is a young gay man so it's hard for me to imagine that he was unfamiliar with the feeling of half-dried lube.

2 More Shades Of Red

Just when you think you've hit rock bottom in terms of embarrassment, you have another adventure in humiliation. The audition notice said "comedians wanted." I went and did some comedy. They laughed. Hard. I even used a new joke about my new, super gay underwear. I was pleased.

They asked me if I sing or dance or play an instrument and I said no.

Why is it that people never believe you when you say you can't dance?

They asked us to stick around for a minute, and then one of the folks whispered to me, "If you want to stretch out a little bit the choreographer wanted to see how you would learn one of our steps."

There was no back door.

So I went on stage and attempted to "learn some steps." That is, dance.

After about forty-five seconds they cut the music. "Okay, we've seen enough."

I told them I couldn't dance.

I can write jokes. I can make excellent vegetarian chili and really good cheesy eggs. I can do a 360 on my skateboard and I am very good at giving intramuscular injections, even to screaming, kicking children. I can figure out pubic transportation in almost any city.

But really, it's true. I can't dance.61 Pink Shirts
The university gig was scheduled to begin at 9 o'clock. At 8:55 p.m. a huge group of young women walked in, as a pack, and sat down, a phalanx of pink t-shirts. As I was introduced and began to perform, it became clear that these girls were on an outing. And not just any outing, an outing as part of a sorority pledge week.

There was nothing to do but call the moment. About three minutes into it I asked "Did you guys mean to come to this event? I was scheduled by the LGBT office. I'm a queer stand up comic." They all nodded.

Coming to my gig was part of a sorority hazing.

I threw out my set list and began rifling through my mental Rolodex of my material. There were people who sat kind of speechless and at least two girls who made little "ew, that's gross" faces at each other, but they were a very small minority.

Considering that in the panel before my performance, someone actually laughed out loud when a panelist referred to "people of all genders, since I believe there aren't just two" and there was a lengthy discussion of whether feminists could wear miniskirts, I felt like I got off easy.

At the end of the performance, the pink t-shirts girls asked if we could take a picture together, and the girl standing next to me said, "Oh, I'm by Kelli," and put her arm around me for the picture.

As they left, one of them said to me, "I'm so glad we were able to come hear you speak. It was either this or drink beer out of each other's vaginas."

I think I'm really funny and all, but I'd have to think twice about those choices. And I don't even like beer.

0 Times

Zero is the number of times my girlfriend let me get into the hot tub when I was accidentally booked at a gay resort for bear weekend. When we checked in, the front desk person gave us a map that showed the safe places to have public sex. My girlfriend said, "I don't think this was meant for us," and tried to give it back.

I pulled her hand down. "Honey, no one ever hands a couple of dykes a map with suggested places to have public sex. This is a once in a lifetime opportunity."

We made use of the map, but she wouldn't let me use the hot tub. I pestered her about it while we perused a flea market in the rural area near the inn.

"First of all, it's going to be full of hair," she said, "and second, it's going to be full of cum."

"We can shower afterward," I argued.

She stared at me. "What if some sperm gets in your vagina and you get pregnant? Then what?"

"If I get pregnant with some hot tub bear's cum baby I will consider it a gift from the baby Jesus and raise it as my own," I said.

I said this apparently too loudly, because now other people were staring at us. We decided it was a good time to leave the flea market.

10 Seconds

Ten seconds is the average time between entering a female bathroom on the road, especially on a New Jersey, and the time someone tries to steer me into another bathroom. I have two new techniques for dealing with bathroom gender policing:

#1. I do an explanation of my gender that is so long, complicated, and full of gender studies jargon that the bathroom police will not engage in bathroom policing in the future unless they know they have a good thirty minutes to kill. If necessary, I will follow them out of the bathroom to continue the explanation. For good measure, I quote Leslie Feinberg, S. Bear Bergman, Kate Bornstein, The Bible and Winnie the Pooh.

#2. I regale them with spontaneous slam poetry. "You can't tell if I am a girl or boy / but you should know I am not your toy / you wear a black hat and faded blue jeans / but you should know I am not unclean." I make sure to use the word oppress/ion split over two lines, as required by standards from the National Association for Queer Slam Poetry.

Two Tits, Take One
Two is the number of breasts I showed at the at two Portland shows. I think I might like performing topless. Not every time, I don't want to get a reputation as a topless comic, but I like that people have to see and deal with my freaky body. And for real, I'd like to be a role model for masculine of center people to get naked, tits and all. If they want to. Or at least get a mammogram.

Two Tits, Take Two
I was emceeing at the Sisterspace Weekend night stage, in addition to doing a thirty-minute set. When my set was over, I introduced my friend Kali who was going to be doing a "reclaiming sexuality" performance ritual. As I was walking off stage she asked, "Can you stay and give me a hand?"

I'm Sister Mary Helpypants, so I did. Because I am of the short haired queer breed, usually when someone asks me for a favor it involves picking up something heavy or using tools, neither of which I have a particularly knack for, although I am always willing to try.

I was apparently even less talented at what Kali wanted me to do, which was to participate in a group strip tease. On stage. To music. I wasn't even really going to attempt it, but once women started coming up from the audience and there was every imaginable size shape and age of naked body on display, I realized I would look like the world's worst spoilsport if I just stood there stubbornly with my arms crossed.

I started taking my clothes off and folding them in a pile at my feet, just like I do when I take off my clothes to get ready for bed. As it turns out, this is not how a striptease is done. Apparently one of the most important parts of a strip tease is the throwing of the clothes.

"Throw them, don't fold them, throw them," Kali urged, and I began throwing my clothes, in the manner I was most familiar. Overhand. Like a baseball.

Despite initial reluctance and the curve ball I'd had to handle with the whole throwing business, I managed to get all my clothes off before the song was over. When the music was done and all the other dancers scrambled for their clothes, I realized why they had been using a dainty underhand throw. It was not merely for aesthetic reasons: it was a question of trajectory and perhaps more importantly, distance.

In the time it took my compatriots to gather all their clothes, I found exactly one single brown sock. Which I put on, because that's a sexy look. It was time for me to introduce the next act which I was thinking was a girl with a guitar who would take only a moment to plug in. After that, I figured, I could run off stage and search for the rest of my garments.

Such was not the case. The next act was Bitch & Animal and they had kettle drums, harps, violins, french horns, and a huge Ghanian Xylophone to set up. I was forced to be onstage for twenty minutes, vamping while wearing nothing but one brown sock.

Although the audience was not at all distracted by my naked form, I was very much so. I stuttered around for a minute or two until I had the idea of doing all the material I performed in my earlier set, but doing it this time with one breast talking to another.

Another 1 Bites the Dust

Walking onto the stage for a show in Portland I totally bit it. Meaning, I fell all the way to the floor. I just took a bow and got up and then started my set. I was carrying a glass of water which went all over the floor but since I still held on to it, didn't break. Jessica Halem, one of the other comics got napkins and started mopping it up and also, with extreme compassion, assuaged my wounded pride by whispering encouragement in my ear as I walked off stage.

I asked a friend later what I tripped on. She replied, "Your big butch ego."

32 Prides

Thirty-two is the number of prides that the anti-gay group Repent America protested at in June of 2003.

I'm a big queer stand up comic and I only performed at twelve. They were protesting at the first pride I ever performed at, in Philadelphia. Their group stood less than a foot away from the stage.

It must have been National Yell The Obvious Through A Megaphone Day, because the lead homophobe kept screaming, "You're a dyke! You're a big fat dyke!"

I leaned over and simultaneously whispered into his ear and the mic. "Dude, I know I'm a dyke. I have a mirror at home."

The lead homophobe of Repent America has a full beard,

a belly and always wears a black leather bar vest. He looks like he got lost on the way to the bear bar. Which is probably pretty much what happened.

1 Humiliating Experience(s) in Lack of Pop Culture Knowledge

I was emceeing Seattle Pride, and introduced Crystal Waters as a drag queen.

2 or 3 Things I Know For Sure

When I was on *Penn and Teller's Bullshit* talking about my experience with the Missionaries of Charity I realized two things: Americans love TV, and they hate dykes who say mean things about nuns.

It seems that the Americans who love TV and hate dykes who say mean things about nuns the most, also have the most time on their hands and the most unfettered access to a computer.

And also, apparently, least access to spellcheck. I didn't even know dyke could be spelled with so many *I*'s. As a friend pointed out, they probably meant something more like "*Diiiiiiiiiiiiiiiiiiiiiiiiiiiiiiiiiike!!!*" as it might sound if yelled from a car window.

My favorite piece of *Penn and Teller* fan mail came from a nice lady named Tina (spelled with just one I, as far as I know) from Idaho who thought I should "shut up" because I am a "freak of nature." Oh Tina, you don't know me, you don't know my family, or you would realize I am a freak of *nurture*.

3 Email Exchanges

When I was preparing for my southern comedy tour, I was delighted by the fan mail I received. And by "fan mail" I mean "vaguely threatening online missive."

It seems that one Paul J. Mitchell[*] took issue with my Radical Queer Agenda posting on the Nashville Craigslist event forum. In response to "LGBT and need to laugh?" Mr. Crankypants wrote:

Stay the hell away from Nashville. I hate queers.

I felt ambivalent about how to respond to this email. As a Master of Bad Ideas (this is not an exaggeration: I got sick from dollar store sardines, not one time, but twice) this struck me as a teachable moment. I mulled over the possible options.

Perhaps Mr. Mitchell just needed to see some queer stand up comedy and he would find that he loves queers. In which case I should offer to comp him into the show.

Perhaps Mr. Mitchell is trying to express his ambivalence at the perils of the rigid gender binary but lacks the vocabulary to do so. In which case I should suggest he come to the next event at the Center for Lesbian and Gay Studies, loan him my copy of *Stone Butch Blues* or perhaps invite him to brunch with my friends.

Or, more likely, Mr. Mitchell is a predominantly heterosexually identified cis dude who finds himself attracted to chubby boi dykes. In which case, I could respond, as I do to indications of sexual interest from men on the street. That is, by saying, "If you're sexually attracted to me, you know that means you're totally gay, right?"

Instead I responded thus:

Dear Mr Mitchell:

I am sorry to hear you hate queers. I get what you're saying. I totally hate brussel sprouts. Recently I found; however, that it makes my life easier to just avoid places where brussel sprouts congregate instead of insisting that brussel sprouts

---

[*] ::cough:: gay name ::cough::

avoid me. You would not believe how much time this saves me on email.

With much affection,
Kelli the Comic

It's hard to overestimate the usefulness of a good solid brussel sprouts analogy.

Mr Mitchell wrote me back that very afternoon.

The last thing I want is lgbt affection

So I friended him on Facebook.

7 People

Seven is the number of people in the audience when I performed in a Nashville, Tennessee Anarchist Performance Collective. It was raining, the roof was leaking. Something smelled like a dead rat. It was most likely a dead rat.

Besides the event's producer and her partner, the only people in attendance were my sister Patt, my old friend Sideshow Bennie, a dude who makes his living pounding nails into his head, and Sideshow Bennie's wife. I can't imagine what they found to talk about but my sister Patt The Accountant and Sideshow Bennie and his wife all had plenty of time to chat before the show, since things at the Anarchist Performance Collective did not start on time.

The performance itself was a bit of a bust but two things came out of that night: my sister learned what an anarchist is ("a libertarian that doesn't bathe") and she and Sideshow Bennie are now Facebook friends.

4 People

Four is the number of people on the Greyhound Bus from Nashville, Tennessee to Huntsville, Alabama. Three guys just getting out of prison, and me. I knew they were just getting out of prison because as they got on the bus they said, "Hey! We're just getting out of prison!"

When they saw me, they were elated and said, "There's a chick on this bus."

I laughed and told them, "I am sincerely sorry that you have been deprived of female companionship for such a long time and now there is a chick on your bus but that chick is me."

100 percent

The percentage of people on my Southern tour who fancied themselves comics. While loading onto a bus on my DC to Knoxville leg I accidentally handed the driver my folded up set list instead of my itinerary.

He looked over the piece of paper for a full thirty seconds while I slowly realized my mistake.

"I don't know where you're trying to go with this, " he said dryly, handing it back to me, "but I'm almost positive Megabus can't take you there."

38 Minutes

At a road gig in a certain Florida city I was booked for a show that was slated to begin at 10:30 p.m., but didn't get started until almost 11:55. Perhaps I should have taken this an omen: 11:55 is way past my bedtime.

Additionally, the audience members were substantially inebriated and although each of them had paid a significant cover, ostensibly to see me perform, they were much more interested in playing bar games. They were entertaining themselves with the old standbys like, "let's see who can talk the loudest," and, "let's see who can get intoxicated and fall off their chair first," and my personal favorite, "let's see who can spew drunken vomit closest to the stage."

Such a situation is not completely unheard of in the roving queer comedy world, and is often easily overcome with sheer volume. This is because as the performer, you have access to a microphone attached to a sound system that enables you to draw attention to yourself and then use your abundant wit and humor to distract the audience from the above-mentioned games. You can then provide the show you are being paid to provide.

All this presupposes something very important. The presence of a working microphone.

Having a working microphone is written into my contract, as well as something I specifically mention in the preliminary emails with a venue and the first thing I check out when I arrive in a venue. Still, the mic that night worked approximately half the time. Unfortunately even when the mic was working, I could neither speak louder than a whisper nor stray from a one square foot area of the stage without the mic producing an ear shattering feedback squeal.

I asked the venue manager to fix the sound system but they couldn't, and my request for a back-up mic was met with a very blank stare. I never had control of the audience no matter what I did. I tried political material. I tried sexual material. I laid down on the stage. I did push-ups on the stage. I walked out into the crowd and sat on the laps of strangers.

Finally, thirty-eight minutes into the show, I left the mic on the stage, walked into the crowd, sat down next to an audience member. I asked to borrow her lit cigarette, inhaled and promptly fell into paroxysms of coughing. The audience interpreted this as a cleverly executed bit of slapstick humor. However, because before that moment I had never taken a single drag from a single cigarette, the coughing fit was not realistic, but real.

Thirty-eight minutes into a sixty minute set, I got the only laugh of the night.

101 Questions

A few years ago, I got an email from someone whose email signature included the phrase "Lead/Business Analyst Global UAT/North America UAT."

These words were utterly incomprehensible to me.

She said, "I am a member of BigCreditCardCompany's Diversity Council and we are working on activities/events in recognition of June's GLBT month." She then asked me if I ever do corporate gigs and what my prices are.

Of course, I said, "Yes, my specialty is corporate gigs," which is technically true, because my specialty is defined as, "any gig that pays me in more than frequent flyer miles and lube."

We sent a few emails back and forth about possible presentations (I was pushing for "LGBT 101") until she wrote me, quite lathered up: "Our committee had to give your information over to our HR department. They have to make sure nothing is going to be offensive, gay or straight. We are thinking about LGBT 101, this seems to be the one we think would not offend anyone."

From past experience I knew that "LGBT 101" probably would offend at least one person. Not because I was going to be extolling the virtues of buttsex in graphic detail, but because some people are offended by the idea that queer relationships are equal to straight ones. However, I tactfully explained that I did indeed know how to present material in a "non-offensive" way, that is by staying within the commonly accepted guidelines for "corporate clean."

I explained that this would nevertheless not guarantee that no one would be offended.

Her next email contained her idea of a solution, "We will

have our HR head and the head of our Regional Operations present, just to make sure if something appears to be going in the wrong direction, they will just signal for you to move on."

What, exactly, did they think I was going to do? Say dirty words? Show dirty pictures? Tear pages from the Bible and wipe my ass with them?

I did like that I was their first exposure to queerness. *Me!* I was the representative of our species!

I could just imagine the dinnertime sharing of any random employee of BigCreditCardCompany, "Guess what came to our office today! A genderqueer! I had never seen one that close up before. Not in the wild! Apparently they are usually very short, often with exceptionally short legs, and they have extremely short hair. And they are a little socially awkward and they like to read books and eat macaroni and cheese and use the word *folks* when they mean *people*."

23 Panicked Emails

BigCreditCardCompanies in the northeast and nursing schools in Sioux City, Iowa have something in common: they panic when forced to deal with a real, live homosexual.

Here's a little tip for you, if you work for a homophobic Catholic college. You might want to search for an image of the performer before, rather than after, the contract is signed.

Once the staff of the Midwestern nursing school discovered just how gay I looked, I was subjected to a barrage of emails from their director of student activities, a frightened descendant of Paul Revere, "The lesbian is coming! The lesbian is coming!"

One email asked me to cover all visible tattoos. I guess the invisible ones I could leave uncovered? And c'mon I'm just a dorky boi dyke. I like to read books and play board games. It's not like my tattoos are stylized mutilated naked women or a Tasmanian devil eating a child. My tattoos are of dolphins, and a bunny rabbit and the Virgin Mary.

They also asked me to refrain from using any "barnyard" language. I had fantasies of opening up my power point presentation and flipping almost silently through each slide, only occasionally breaking the quiet with a random "moo" and "baaaaaaa."

Their final email before I arrived reminded me not to mention any specific sexual acts during my performance. I was contracted to provide a humorous presentation called the *ABCs of Surviving Nursing School.* Where exactly I would think that within that presentation a reference to say, anal fisting would be needed is still a mystery to me.

17 Pets

There were seventeen pets in attendance at a fundraiser I performed in at Ginger's, an old school Park Slope Lesbian Bar.

I only knew after they booked me that it was a fundraiser for a gay animal shelter. I assume it was a shelter for animals who identified as gay since "gay-run animal shelter" seems redundant. I've never been around any group of folks trying to help out stray cats where the homos were not over-represented.

Since it was a fundraiser for gay animals, the gay animals apparently came out to support. I was trying out some new material and I couldn't believe how great the audience response was, until I turned around to see they were reacting not to my hilarity, but to the hilarity of a Great Dane who was sniffing my ass.

5 Minutes

One of my favorite road trip hotel hobbies is participating in conference activities with which I am not affiliated. The prizes are the free food and drink, as well as the excitement of seeing how long I can make conversation about GRE scores or camping licenses or recreational theory. The game is over when I am found out or when it becomes obvious to me that I will be found out in the next few moments and it becomes too uncomfortable for me to continue my charade.

The shortest time at an UHA (unaffiliated hotel activity): Five minutes at the Coordinating Group on Cape Cod Non-Native Aquatic Pest Species. (Cape Codder Resort, Hyannis MA).

The longest time at UHA: 47 minutes at the Anderson Family Reunion. A lot of nodding, as well as agreeing that Aunt Penny was a bad driver got me through a plate of ribs and two diet cokes.

43 Years, 59 Hours

I was forty-three years old when I started my Good Ol' Fashioned Queer Comedy Revival Show Southern Tour during which I spent no less than fifty-nine hours riding 3360 miles on buses through the south. I'm took seventeen different Megabus rides, plus local transportation, and performed seven times in six different cities in six extremely different venues, including a community center, a church, a converted barn.

When I told my mom about my plan to spend two weeks touring via Megabus, she was a little confused.

I ended up yelling "No no no, not a tour bus." I wasn't yelling because I was angry but because I was on the phone with my mom and was therefore, as per usual, competing with the musical intro to the Gaither Family Gospel Show. I remember The Gaither's show well and even fondly from childhood, but it is not easy to have a conversation over it.

"Not a tour bus mom," I repeated, "I'm going to be taking a Megabus."

She had never heard of a Megabus and thought it was a description rather than a brand. She was probably hoping I'd be touring through the South on a triple-long, triple-wide mega sized bus that has its own swimming pool, resident cat, and a big huge refrigerator built especially to keep my Diet Mountain Dew cool.

"No it's just the name of specific public bus. Like Greyhound."

My mom was silent for a moment and then she said the words she has learned to say when she doesn't know what to say. "Well that sounds." Beat. "Interesting."

I know my mom well enough to know when her inflection on "interesting" means "bananas."

She's not the first person to suggest that maybe this tour is a little *interesting*.

When I explained to another queer performer that I'd be taking to the road for two weeks, entirely on public transportation, they looked at me sideways. "Isn't that something you do in the beginning of your career? You know, when you're in your 20's."

"In my 20's I was a nun," I explained, "and the sisters frowned on taking time off from the soup kitchen to go on queer comedy tours."

12 Straight People

It is not easy to attract an audience when you're competing with Margaret Cho and Kate Clinton and someone dressed up like Cher on a scooter. When our ad hoc comedy team *Famous Lesbian Comedy Roadshow (Famous Lesbians Not Included)* did a week in Provincetown we spent all afternoon every afternoon trying to convince vacationing queers of our collective hilarity. We'd walk from couple to couple offering Hershey Kisses and a postcard saying "funny lesbians, free chocolate."

After a few less than stellar crowds, my two fellow performers headed back to their hotel rooms and announced, as if this were the obvious next step, that it was time to break out the costumes.

I was confused. Costumes? I didn't even know we were required to travel with costumes.

Twenty minutes later, they emerged, Elizabeth in homemade Wonder Woman attire and Katie in homemade Xena garb. I put on the closest thing I had to a costume, a clean t-shirt and a pair of cargo shorts.

We were walking down Commercial Street, flyering people within an inch of their lives, when a large group of straight people crossed the road. Their patriarch turned, gazed at us and made the common straight person mistake: assuming that because he was surrounded by gays that he truly understands them.

The patriarch turned to his second in command and pointed at my friends in their Wonder Woman and Xena garb.

"See them," he said with the air of authority that comes only with being a white cisgender straight man opining on a subject about which he knows nothing. "Those are two men."

His second-in-command nodding sagely, pointed at me in my t-shirt and cargo shorts and added, "Look closely, that third one's a drag queen too."

Yes, yes I'm a drag queen. I'm the world's laziest drag queen. I'm a drag queen that can't be bothered to make any changes to my personal appearance so that I make the slightest resemblance to stereotypical femininity. I'm a drag queen that wears a sports bra. I'm a drag queen that sometimes wears as many as four sports bras at a time.

For real, if you see a drag queen wearing a sports bra? Call 911 and take her to the nearest hospital emergency room because she is most certainly not well.

1 Clothed Performer

I got booked at a lesbian night at a local strip club. I had never done the strip club thing and didn't find it particularly sexy but it was super fun listening to friends' commentary on the super athletic moves of the dancers. Flipping over backwards, essentially throwing themselves at the pole, and then holding their bodies out from the pole and wiggling. These were the girls who were really good at the flexed arm hang in school.

Although it seemed like women were tipping pretty consistently and having a good time, it was also very much a social occasion so when they turned off the music and there were no more nearly naked women doing extremely athletic moves on the stage, everyone took it as their cue to chat.

But their cue to chat was my cue to go on stage.

Somewhat overconfident, I thought I should imitate some of the dancers.

"I don't get it, how did these women figure out they could do these moves. How does someone know they can crawl and shake their ass at the same time. For example, I can crawl." It occurs to me to demonstrate this to the crowd, forgetting that it's been a long time since I've crawled in public, plus I have a mic in my hand. Plus I am also over forty years old and have over forty style joints.

By the time I thought of that I was already on the stage on all fours imitating myself not being a stripper.

Getting up, I tore my medial collateral ligament in my right knee in the process.

How I really wanted to end the joke was by adding, "but I can't crawl and wiggle my ass at the same time," while I while was on all fours doing just that.

However since I had incapacitating pain shooting up and down my right leg, I decided to forgo the acting out of the joke and just say the line. And then get the hell off the stage before I started to cry.

1 Question

Like most independent artists, I am uninsured, but I live in the great city of New York where entertainment professionals can get free primary care at the Al Hirschfeld Health Clinic. The clinic is located in a building that provides housing for middle income retired entertainment professionals, so when you get in the elevator, you will inevitably recognize at least one other passenger, usually from a supporting role in a 70's sitcom.

The doctor there only sees entertainers all day, every day. When I hurt my knee imitating a stripper on stage he didn't ask, "Why on earth were you imitating a stripper on stage?" Instead he asked, "Is imitating a stripper on stage something you'll need to do on an ongoing basis to maintain your livelihood?"

I really do love New York.

(Dis)Honoring Columbus

Some of my siblings escaped Hartford, Wisconsin through the military. When I graduated from high school, no one even so much as hinted that I might want to join the army. I was the youngest of seven kids, and a complete temperament mismatch with my family. While the rest of my siblings were of the stoic Germanic stock so common and needed in farming Wisconsin, I emerged fully formed from the womb, a whiny sensitive queer.

When it rained, I would miss the bus trying to save the worms that crawled out onto the pavement, returning them to the grass to save them from being run over. According to my cousins, this was not the kind of behavior encouraged at boot camp.

I spent exactly one disastrous semester at Bible College. An adult from the church I attended mentioned that her brother, a veterinarian working in Haiti, had heard there was a school for kids with orthopedic disabilities in Port-au-Prince that desperately needed volunteers.

"They just need someone to help out with recreation for the kids in the afternoon," he had explained, "no special skills needed."

It seemed like in a situation of desperate need that required no special skills, I couldn't help but be useful, even it were accidentally. I mentioned the idea to my mother. "Well, you are a helpypants," she said, with that mixture of respectful hands-off parenting and understated sarcasm that my mom has honed to an art form. It was the closest I was going to get to a parental blessing.

I wrote a letter to Sister Joan, the head of the school, and saved money from my summer camp job to buy a plane ticket. That was the sum total of my preparation.

When I arrived at the school Sister Joan was ensconced in her small office, the only room with air conditioning on the entire campus. She motioned to the seat beside her and said, "First of all, you need to get your hair cut. I can't see your eyes." I only nodded, confused by the implication that I was some kind of hippie flouting the establishment instead of a scared 18-year-old with a bad spiral perm.

"Second, you have to keep your eyes on these people," she said, "they lie and cheat and steal."

And so in one sentence, I learned that Sister Joan, the seventy-eight-year-old Episcopal nun who had been running St. Vincent's School for forty years, was both a bully and a bigot.

The first week I taught the kids to make paper airplanes, which they immediately used to pelt each other in the head. Considering the limited supplies and my even more limited knowledge of arts and crafts, it was probably one of my most successful lessons.

I learned Kreyol on the job, from the kids. I recommend this method of instruction if you want to learn a language both very quickly and very badly. Whenever I asked the kids how to say something, they would always pick the most vulgar word that more or less meant was I was saying, often passing off fully disgusting idioms as if they were sacred Haitian proverbs.

I had big ideas. I wanted to learn how to speak so I could discuss philosophy, religion, and politics with my new friends. But since kids were my teachers, one of the first sentences I learned was not something interesting such as, "Shall we engage in a conversation about the politics of meta-preferences?" Nor was it something useful like, "I feel very vulnerable on the street with all this shooting. May I please step inside your house?" Instead, one of the first phrases I learned in Kreyol was the kind small children love to bandy around on the playground: *Gro mal rat, ou santi mayas.* Roughly translated this means: You are a big awful rat. And your feet stink.

In addition, learning language from children presented another problem. Occasionally the kids, bored with being uncompensated Kreyol instructors, would tell me that a word or phrase meant something very different than what it actually did.

This led to some rather interesting situations, for example, when I went to a small café beside the school and thought I was asking for a "cold coke" when in reality I was asking, apparently in a rather vulgar way, to see a private part of the waiter's male anatomy. That same week, when I was attempting to quell the mass chaos that was erupting among the children as we practiced for the school play I thought I was saying, "Everyone please listen." I actually said, much to the children's delight, "Everyone please spit."

They of course, complied.

Even now, more than twenty years later, occasionally an adult will blanch at my choice of vocabulary. I've learned to immediately backtrack. "I'm sorry, I learned Kreyol from children. Could you please tell me the more polite way to say that?"

Sister Joan had not been wrong when she said they "desperately needed" volunteers. The kids, who mostly came in from provinces to the only school that would take kids with orthopedic disabilities, were very overcrowded in their dorms and very bored. After 3:30 p.m., when classes were done, it was not unusual to turn the corner and find two kids, each hopping on one foot, while they attempted to beat the other with a prosthetic leg. These prosthetics were not slender blades of titanium made for running in the Olympics, they were heavy duty wood prostheses appropriate for village life and climbing up the side of deforested mountains. Beating your classmates with them was not a safe activity.

Providing recreation was almost a defensive act.

Although I tried to help the kids have fun that wouldn't result in broken limbs, I was overwhelmed, inexperienced, and frequently out of ideas. We didn't have many supplies and the ages of the kids ranged from four to nineteen years. I was impatient and too often short with them.

I also managed to contract ringworm on my face which I ignored until the fungus covered one entire cheek and people began assuming it was a scar from a car accident. It itched constantly and so I would rub my face, especially when I was thinking of a word, which was all the time.

The kids started calling me *gratay blan*, or "the scratching white person."

Things were going great.

One morning a few months after my reign as Hapless Recreation Volunteer began, Sister Joan summoned me into her office. "I have a very special project for you. The children must do a play about Christopher Columbus. They should know more about the heroes of Haiti."

I tried to reason with the severely misinformed nun but she simply told me to leave.

I knew I couldn't make them do it. I might not be able to teach those kids to latch-hook or how to fold paper lanterns or play soccer, true. But I refused to force them to spend a third of the school year artistically celebrating centuries of greed and genocide.

That afternoon I grabbed five of the oldest kids and took them to an empty classroom to explain the situation. We were all silent, just a bunch of hot, angry teenagers, stewing in our grumbling resentment.

After some time one of the kids got up and began the most favorite of Saint Vincent pastimes: physically imitating another kid's disability. As Noel, who was partially sighted, pretended to be a blind classmate, stumbling around, dramatically bumping into walls and falling over, another kid said, "Oh look, it's Christopher Columbus discovering Haiti by accident."

With that, we had the start of our script. The kids wrote a play that was something between a classic farce and a Saturday Night Life sketch. Christopher Columbus became a bumbling character, landing in Haiti, falling off his boat and squishing three small children in the process. He never walked into the room without tripping over something.

They built a huge paper maché goat, which a kid would throw through the scene whenever Columbus spoke, in a particularly jarring attempt at establishing an objective correlative. The implication, I guess, was that his voice was so grating that it caused even farm animals to run or even fly in potentially suicidal horror.

The Haitian staff would occasionally stop in for rehearsals, shake their hands and laugh. Although Sister Joan would sometimes ask how the play was going, I always nodded and gave her the thumbs up. I'd never crossed her before, so she had no reason to question further. And while I was still afraid of making her angry, I certainly couldn't imagine stopping the joy I was watching unfold before me.

On the day of the play's debut, the parents who lived in town filed in and Sister Joan sat in the front row. The kids were so excited that every bit of physical comedy they had rehearsed was magnified threefold. Christoper Columbus tripped four times in each scene. He nearly squished five small children when he fell out of his boat. The objective correlative goat flew so hard and so fast—accompanied by desperate soulful bleating sounds—that it would often crash into the opposite wall.

There was also a surprise ending that the kids had written the night before, informed by an incident in the most recent coup, when a mob ripped out a thirty foot high statute of Columbus from in front of the National Palace, carried it to the port and dumped it in the ocean. As the kid playing Christopher Columbus said his last line, the entire cast rushed him, hustled him from the room and pushed him into the therapy pool just outside. The crowd cheered, the kids looked deliriously happy, and Sister Joan barely spoke to me for the next five months.

It was totally worth it.

Years later, I was chatting with an older Haitian gentleman I met on the bus in Brooklyn about downtown Port-au-Prince and what it was like "back then."

We talked about St. Vincent's, about some of the stores, about what the streets were like at night. A bit confused by my time-specific knowledge, and unsure of my chronological age, he asked, "Wait, did you grow up there?"

I had to smile at his question.

"A little bit. I grew up just a little bit there."

Degaje

Degaje: In Haitian Kreyol, roughly translated, means "to get along" especially to get along with a not-quite-official work around.

Prologue: Racism's Greatest Hits, January 14, 2010

In the very short burst of media attention that followed Haiti post-earthquake, the Onion had some of the most honest coverage of any American news source. The headline in the January 25 issue of the satirical paper read: Massive Earthquake Reveals Entire Island Civilization Called 'Haiti.' The caption under a rubble-filled photo: "Americans laid eyes on actual Haitians for the first time on Jan. 12"

Mainstream news coverage of Haiti has frequently made me want to gouge out my eyes with an auger. Articles about Haiti, even in major newspapers, still use the judgmental word "squalor" with such gleeful abandon one wonders if the National Association of Citizens to Encourage Racism is offering a reward for each utterance.

The media serves up images of Haiti like a morbid all-you-can-consume misery buffet. That so many died is no "natural" disaster. It is the result of years of poverty that has been systematically ignored and in many cases contributed to, by policies of the US and other "developed" nations. I wish every single one of those images of suffering were accompanied with a bottom of screen crawl: "this is what racism looks like."

Post-earthquake, every available journalist reported to Haiti, eager to make a name for themselves amidst the aforementioned squalor. Based on that coverage, I'm 99.5% percent sure the following handout was issued to anyone with a press pass as they entered Port-au-Prince in January 2010.

Dear Journalist,

Welcome to hell! As you know, White People have a long proud history of misunderstanding Haiti and it's important that we maintain the mainstream media's high standard of wanton misrepresentation in order to maintain this tradition. Please observe the following guidelines when preparing your reports:

#1. Do not under any circumstances bother to learn the name of the neighborhood you're reporting from. The generic term "Port-au-Prince slum" will work fine, especially since "slum" has no precise meaning or purpose beyond othering the area.

#2. Please make sure to proclaim a specific area "devastated" by the earthquake without looking at any "before" pictures to see if this description is accurate. Your readers might otherwise be reminded that we've been ignoring how bad things are in Haiti for a while now.

#3. It's very important that you describe expressions of sorrow in their most extreme physical manifestations. This helps with the essential othering process mentioned in Guideline #1.

#4. Photographers must always show white people calm and black people not calm.

#5. An important note about photos: the more the subject in a photograph is suffering, the closer the shot should be.

If you encounter a person who is very close to death and is, for example, screaming in pain, the camera lens should actually touch their face.

#6. Anyone who eats food procured in any way other than having a white person hand it to them should be referred to as a "looter." These same people should be described as "traveling Port-au-Prince slums in lawless gangs" even if they're just a family out searching for drinking water.

#7. On-air reporters: DO NOT ever interview a Haitian about the situation on the ground. Obviously, as the people living through the tragedy, they are unable to be objective and are not reliable sources of information. White people are more reliable. Ideally, locate a white celebrity.

#8. Photojournalists must never show black people rescuing other black people from destroyed buildings as these are likely only accidental findings that happen in the context of looting. Photos of white people rescuing black people are permissible, with priority given to photos in which the rescuee is naked, crying, so hurt as to be unable to participate in their rescue in any way, or otherwise exceptionally vulnerable. Haitians should not be shown demonstrating self-agency or self-help as this will just confuse your readers.

#9. If you must interview a Haitian because no white people are available, under no circumstances should you interview someone who speaks only Kreyol, since any translator available is likely to be a Haitian and again, not reliable. In addition, interviews in Kreyol dangerously imply that English is not the superior language and that the information local people provide might possibly be important.

#10. You must never never never never provide any historical context for Haiti's poverty. Especially do not mention that every slave holding country refused to trade with Haiti for decades after their revolution, the twenty-year

American occupation, or the US part in the coup that ousted democratically-elected president Jean Bertrand Aristide. If one of these topics inadvertently is brought up, such as by an interview subject, immediately change the subject to voodoo or AIDS.

#11. Remember the phrase "life is cheap here" because you will need it in order to dismiss the death toll. After all, hundreds of people are being buried in mass graves and starving relatives of the deceased continue to look for food, how upset can they really be? It's obvious that Haitians don't mourn for the people they love like normal people because *life is cheap here*. See how that works?

#12. The White People From Rich Countries Law requires that the word "hovel" must be used within ten words of the first mention of the proper nouns "Haiti," or "Haitians." Failure to observe this convention can lead to severe penalties, including not being eligible for the Pulitzer Prize.

#13. Media coverage of Haiti should be discontinued two weeks after the tragedy or in the event of a drunken Lindsay Lohan sighting, whichever comes first. Continuing to generate copy or taking photographs after this time is at your own risk and expense, since no media outlet will publish it after the expiration date of White People's Attention.

Getting There Is Half The Fun
My girlfriend Cheryl said she had two thoughts when she heard about the earthquake in Haiti. First, "Those poor people do not need this," and second, "Kelli is definitely going to want to go." She was right about both thoughts.

Immediately after the quake, I spent hours on conference calls with clueless relief agencies. On one conference call, a nurse expressed reservations about going to Haiti if she would not be allowed to practice within her specialty.

After more than ten days of trying to find some agency who was looking for a Kreyol speaking nurse to help out for a few weeks, I talked with my long time friend John who is an American nurse practitioner living in Port-au-Prince. I first met him there in 1987.

"Oh just get yourself here," he said. "We'll find you someplace to work."

Helpful hint: If you ever find yourself struggling to get to a country devastated by a natural disaster and you finally figure out your plan? Tell your girlfriend before you announce it on Facebook.

The suggestion "just get yourself here" was a great one to hear but a difficult one to follow. Commercial flights were still not landing in Haiti, since the air traffic systems at the capital's only airport had been damaged by the quake. I emailed friends, lovers, ex-lovers, strangers, acquaintances, enemies and government officials in an attempt to get on a charter flight.

Finally, after a late night conversation with my host, we decided my best bet was to fly to the Dominican Republic so I'd at least be on the same island as Haiti. New York queers chipped in for my airline ticket, I kissed my reluctantly supportive girlfriend goodbye and took the overnight flight.

"I wish I had brought a pogo stick," I said in the car on the way to airport.

She looked at me, not amused. "Why?"

"So I can hop across the border if I need to."

My girlfriend and my friends who were giving me a ride to the airport all got out of the car to help me with my backpack full of medical supplies. I also carted along a ukulele, which I somewhat inexplicably had decided was of high priority to take on this odyssey, despite having never learned how to play the ukulele.

"Don't make us come get you, boo," said my friend.

Cheryl nodded, hands on her hips. "Don't even think about it."

The Hitchhikers' Guide to the Dominican Republic

It could have been much worse. Before my flight even left JFK, I imposed myself on a group of Haitian-American college students who planned to head to the bus terminal in Santo Domingo and see if they could get on a bus to Haiti. We became a spontaneous team, traveling together the whole way and having as much as fun as we could considering the bus transfer/ride took us nearly twelve hours after having spent four hours on the plane. Luxon, our self-elected but charming leader, declared us a family and collected information so we could friend each other on Facebook later.

Facebook helped that day because I couldn't reach John, who was supposed to come pick me up at the bus terminal in Port-au-Prince. The call wouldn't go through on my cell phone. Through the miracle of modern random technology, however, I could get online with my phone and write on his Facebook wall. Anyone who decided to peruse his wall that afternoon was treated to hourly updates. "Hey John, got the Caribe bus, supposedly leaving at 11 a.m., will let you know when I cross the border," and, "we still haven't crossed the border yet," and, "we're at the border, but we've been sitting here for a couple of hours."

In the end, my seat mate Gregory let me use his phone so I could call John directly. Most of us who were in the roving band were from the New York City area. We all got together for dinner after we got back.

You know who wasn't getting a thank you dinner? The Caribe bus company. They charged twice as much for tickets from Santo Domingo to Port-au-Prince as they did before the quake. Since commercial flights hadn't started yet, the bus was one of very few ways people could get into the country to see their families in the early weeks after the quake. Impressive humanitarian show there, guys.

Sa je pa wè, kè pa tounen

What The Eye Doesn't See, Doesn't Turn the Heart
—Haitian proverb

The day after I arrived in Haiti I went with my friend John to downtown Port-au-Prince to make the arrangements for where I would be working the next few weeks. In addition to figuring out where exactly I would be helping out, I wanted to see the Sans Fil area where I used to live & work, as well as St. Vincent, the school I volunteered at when I first moved to Haiti.

Shit.

We almost couldn't find Sans Fil coming from Delmas, the main street that runs through the city. I knew the neighborhood had changed some since I lived there, but because so many of the buildings I would have used as landmarks didn't look like buildings anymore we had to stop and ask directions a few times. Luckily, the main entrance to Sans Fil is ringed by a good sized open air market that sells a lot of meat and has a rather distinctive smell. That was ultimately the way I figured out where we were.

Because you can't really drive through the market, John stayed in the car and I walked though. I ran into the Jardin family, who I had known when I lived in a small house on the nearby soccer field. The woman recognized me after nearly a decade. She even asked about my roommate, who was also a volunteer with the Missionaries of Charity and became an MC, and stayed. The Jardins said that much of the area was okay, mostly because people had small houses.

Even if they lost a wall they were able to get out onto the

soccer field and be safe. All their extended family that lived in a house downtown died when their house fell.

"At least they were together," Mme Jardin said.

I did not know what to say in response to that. This may well have been the theme of the entire trip. I just agreed, "Yes, together," and added, *"kenbe,"* the Kreyol equivalent of "hang in there."

We walked by the National Palais after visiting with some families in San Fil. The National Palais was part of my daily life when I lived in Port-au-Prince because St. Vincent's was less than three blocks away and I would often go for a walk in the morning and pass by the front gates. In the immediate aftermath of the earthquake it had caved in but had not fallen. The folks living in the tent city opposite it had a front row seat to its slow ongoing collapse. I asked an older dude if it wasn't sad to watch. He said, "No one will die when it falls." Sean Penn's nonprofit began tearing it down in 2012.

We walked over to where St. Vincent was. I didn't recognize it at first. John and I stood for a moment trying to figure out if it was, in fact, St. Vincent. Finally, I asked someone who was walking by. He said we were indeed looking at the remains of the school. I had heard the building was damaged, but that all the kids got out. Several people stopped to chat with us and they said that all the kids hadn't gotten out. They didn't know how many died, just "a lot." That's always the number of people who died at any given place it seemed. *Anpil.* Many.

The older boys lived in a dorm called the Foyer, while the girls and younger kids lived at the main school. The entrance to the Foyer was open and so we peeked in. It was empty except for some guys cleaning up the mess. I explained I used to work there and asked how things were going. Francis, one of the dorm parents appeared and began telling me about what happened there during the earthquake. He pointed to a wheelchair sitting by itself, covered in dust, surrounded by broken concrete blocks. Apparently one of the kids was sitting in the chair under a concrete overhang and was killed immediately. They removed his body for his parents, but no one wanted to touch the chair.

We stood around and talked for a while, Francis told me he lost four brothers in the quake. We talked about how much misery Haiti could withstand. We talked about how long folks had been trapped under the rubble and how many had survived that had been presumed dead. Francis said, "The misery of the Haitian people has made us strong." After a silence, I said, "You know white people. We can't go three days without McDonald's let alone survive under a bunch of rocks."

I held my breath for a moment and everyone in the yard laughed.

Francis told us that two of the boys' bodies were trapped upstairs, that they couldn't get them out, and that their feet were still visible. He asked me if I wanted to see them. I said, "No, thank you," in a way that I hoped was respectful. We shook Francis' hand and he thanked us for stopping by.

He thanked us even though we had done absolutely nothing.

We had listened. It just keep coming back to that. People really need to have their stories heard.

Some Days It's A Field Hospital, Some Days It's A Porch

At the end of my first full day in Haiti, John took me to Heartline, where folks who run a women's self empowerment project had set up a field hospital on a porch where they usually hold sewing classes. In the first few days after the earthquake, they were doing amputations on tabletops. They had limited supplies and limited help. Three weeks post quake they were mostly seeing infected wounds and untreated fractures on both an inpatient (on the porch) and outpatient (in the backyard) basis. John said "I have a Kreyol speaking nurse here," and they put me to work right then.

By three o'clock the next day it felt like I had never done anything in my entire life except treat folks in that outpatient line for *ponsma* (dressing changes). The stories were running together. An older man with an external fixation device on his leg, a young woman in a leg cast, a kid with an abscess on his butt. One man told the whole story of what happened to him the day of the earthquake, in detail that makes my stomach feel funny. He knew his leg was broken, he explains, gesturing to the metal device that is holding his shattered femur together, because when he moved it, it wiggled like a worm.

When the truck came back from picking up the injured from a nearby tent city that afternoon, one of the patients that came with them was KB, an eight-year-old kid, and his mom.

I took off KB's dressing, and he had a five-inch open area on his left thigh. Parts of it were nearly half an inch deep. The pediatrician suggested we try to clean it out and admit him to the hospital until we could find another facility that could do a skin graft for him.

KB and I chatted a little bit. I explained the two of us were a team, working together, and that he should let me know if anything I did hurt him too much. I started to work cleaning out his wound. I sang to him, making up a song about his name rhyming with the sound that animals make. It made sense in Kreyol.

After some time, I realized this kid was not saying *anything*. If you've ever done primary care with young school-age kids, you know that they will tear you apart if you start trying to do some crazy thing like give them an immunization. Once, when giving a first grader a simple MMR vaccination, I was bitten almost badly enough to need stitches. In contrast, KB's stoicism was heartbreaking.

Once I got down to healthy tissue there was no way what I was doing wasn't hurting him. But KB just kept staring ahead. While I worked his mom told me the story of what happened to him. He was buried under rubble for four days, with three other people. He was the only one of them that survived.

I finished up the dressing and the logistics team took him and his mom over to the hospital. When I stopped by on my way to dinner I saw that they had settled in. I told KB he had the best bed in the place, since it was near the door and he could get some breeze, which would help with the mosquitoes. He smiled just a tiny bit.

I hoped soon he would be able to cry a little bit too.

Three days later KB's brother came to visit and he became completely *dezod* (shenanigans). Their favorite trick was to wait until I was doing something like pushing IV meds and then call my name multiple times, urgently. Then, when I stood up to see what they needed, act like they had not called me at all.

The hospital was full of kids, so I found myself saying the stuff anyone says to kids. One afternoon I must have said, "I don't care if he poked you in your skin graft site first," about a dozen times.

The Opposite of First World Problems

The next Wednesday night I was at the field hospital on the porch when a young guy was carried in. He was in from the provinces trying unsuccessfully to find his family after the quake. He got hit by a *tap tap*[*] and had a fracture and some soft tissue injury. He said, "It's not my foot that hurts, it's my heart." Later on when his friends came to pick him up, we were trying to figure out the logistics of his trip home. They were making me crazy because they couldn't make a decision about which transportation to use. We went back and forth a bit and then one of the guards at the front gate turned on a flashlight and I saw their faces better.

I realized, oh these are kids. I asked them how old they were and they ranged from fourteen to seventeen years old. Kids! The guy's family was missing and presumed dead and his friends were the ones with the responsibility of trying to bring him back home. When we finally got the logistics cleared up and he had gone, I thought about my biggest worry at fourteen. Whatever it was, I know it most certainly wasn't, "How can I help my friend, whose whole family just died in an earthquake, get safely home with a newly broken foot?"

The Pain Of Hope Kicks Ass

My third night in Haiti I became an impromptu labor coach. My day job at the time was working with first time new moms, so I had a fair amount of experience with birth. However, I have never been one of those people who say, "Oh my goodness, please let me be present at this delivery, I love the celebration of new life." I am more the kind of person who says, "Yes, certainly if you need me, but it's pretty messy."

I am not so enamored of the baby coming out process.

Heartline usually runs a program for pregnant women. A few weeks after the earthquake, people started to come to the program who were in labor, even people who hadn't

[*] *a Haitian form of public transit, a sort of pickup/bus hybrid*

been a part of the program. This is part of the challenge facing Haiti even now, resources that were stretched super thin before the quake are dental floss thin now. The woman had a place picked out a facility to have her baby, but that hospital was *craze' net* (completely destroyed) before she went into labor.

This is how Fredeline came one late afternoon in February to have her baby with strangers. The baby's father hung out for a while and then took off, as Fredeline predicted because *li pa gen patiense* (he has no patience). And so, labor happened. I was in and out at first and then somehow, I got to play the good cop to the midwives' bad cop (they had to push her to squat, to drink, etc) and I ended up impromptu labor coach.

I am a perennial singer of weird songs, some of my own making. I started singing this song I had learned mostly in Miami, it's sung at demonstrations. The chorus is *nou se yon pep gi gen resistans*. One translation might be, "we are a strong surviving people" and my favorite verse is *nou bite' men nou pa tonbe*, which means, "we trip but we don't fall." This was roughly equivalent to singing "We Shall Overcome" while someone is in labor. Maybe not the most appropriate, but I was making the best of my limited repertoire.

I was also making what I hoped were encouraging comments. "You've done other hard things, you can do this too," and, "you're doing great job, hold on," or, "this is terrible pain but it's not the pain of dying, it is the pain of hope," and other such nonsense. Fredeline began to sing my own words back to me: "no, I can't do this, it's killing me," and, "you're crazy if you think I will live after this, the suffering it too much." And then I sang back to her, "it is terrible, but there is a baby coming. The baby is coming soon."

Fredeline delivered at 9:58 p.m. Within minutes, the brilliant midwife and the labor/delivery nurse who were there had cleaned the baby up and Fredeline was successfully breastfeeding him. The baby and Fredeline both did fine.

The pain of hope instead of the pain of dying is a beautiful thing indeed.

Scars

Because of the way buildings fell, especially in the most populated areas of Port-au-Prince, and the time of day of the earthquake, it seemed more children survived than adults. Their smaller size seemed to increase the likelihood that they would survive, since there was less area for falling blocks to make contact. We treated a number of *se li min ki te solve* (he was the only to be saved) kids.

Six-year-old Wesner was one of these children. The first day I arrived in the field hospital I was pushing IV Ancef and trying not to think about how dangerous this practice was when he came to stand beside me. He had a cast on his right leg, a cast on his left arm, and healing lacerations all over as well as a hefty bandage around his head. "I have a problem," he said, literally climbing up my leg, "my mom and dad are dead."

Because he was holding very tightly to me, I had no choice but to let him accompany me while I finished the rest of my work. After a few minutes he added, "and the rest of my family too."

I looked over at the American pediatrician who had gotten there a few days before me. I mouthed, "Everyone in his family is dead?" to her.

She shook her head. "Yes, no, well, no at least he still has his grandma. So there's someone to send him home to when he's better."

Wesner was fascinated by my cover-up tattoo. I have a very large set of scars on my upper left arm from a particularly self-destructive period I went through in my 20's. A decade post aforementioned self-destructive phase, I wanted something to cover up the scars, or at least distract from them. After much contemplation I decided a hippie (not angelic) looking chunky Virgin Mary tattoo would be perfect.

"She needs to look like she shops at Lane Bryant," was how I explained it to the tattoo artist.

Whenever Wesner saw me, he would pull up the arm of my t-shirt and outline this figure with his forefinger, mostly gently, but pressing a little harder in the spots where the tattoo became almost three dimensional, bulging where the skin underneath was deeply scarred.

Every day I would hold him while I drew up meds or whenever I had an extra arm of a free lap and every day he would trace my arm and say *fe sa con sa pou mwen*. Make one like this for me.

I explained to him that I couldn't just walk into a field hospital and give a six-year-old tattoo. I explained to him that I didn't even know how to make tattoos. I explained to him I didn't have the equipment you need. I explained that his scratches and lacerations were still healing.

Still every day he asked.

On my last day at the field hospital I was using a Sharpie to write the change date on an IV bag when I had an idea. I called Wesner over and had him roll up his sleeve. Using the thick blue marker, I drew around the healing areas of his left upper arm, a very rough, free form version of the Virgin Mary.

Wesner could not stop smiling.

Nou blesi menm jan. He said. We have the same wounds.

I felt embarrassed that he had compared my minor post adolescent breakdown with the loss of his entire family, being gravely injured and having to heal in a country impoverished by centuries of racism and colonialism.

But I got what he was saying, so I picked him up and whispered in his ear *Enben, Oke, se vre nou kouvri yo menm jan.*

We definitely cover them up the same way.

Let Us Pray

On the one month anniversary of the earthquake, Haitians were having three days of fasting and prayer. Folks were taking the prayer especially seriously.

The praying was so serious that some patients wouldn't leave church and I did one dressing change during a church service. The kid hadn't left her tent-like structure since she was injured but her family made sure she got to church.

It was hot, and I had to lean over the whole time because there wasn't room to squat. By the time we were done this poor kid had more of my sweat on her than she did of her own.

So much for a sterile field.

On The Truck

Halfway through my four-week stint at the field hospital, the director asked me to start going out with the truck. This meant going out with the truck to the different tent cities and either checking dressings and performing wound care where they were or bringing them in for whatever help they needed.

At one stop where we normally did dressing changes actually on the truck, a doctor took stitches out of a pre-teen boy's recent below knee amputation surgical site. He cried when he saw the instruments.

These kids really learned to hate health care providers.

The kid's grandma was there, since his mom was still in the hospital with injuries sustained in the quake, and she gently held one hand.

"You don't have to look if you're not ready," I reminded him.

As the day continued we loaded up more and more folks onto the truck, including a baby who had been reportedly been having diarrhea for five days. When I picked up the baby to do an assessment, he immediately demonstrated said diarrhea on my shorts, saving me the trouble of asking questions about its color and consistency.

One of the other team members said later, "I never need to hear the words *li fèmal* (it hurts) ever again."

I struggled to be present in the pain. I struggled to keep my brain from scurrying around, trying to create bullshit reasons why this person was different from me, how they were somehow more equipped for this time of misery.

Tomorrow Is Coming

All month I heard people greet one another by saying *demen-ap vini*. Tomorrow is coming.

This was said with an optimistic tone, like, "Fabulous, tomorrow is coming! Something marvelous is probably on its way."

I couldn't help but think that if I had been through what the average person in Haiti went through in January 2010, I would consider "tomorrow is coming" less something to celebrate and more of a threat.

But maybe losing hope is a luxury of folks who have access to clean water and enough to eat.

Clit Teasers

I consider myself an intelligent human being and a competent health care provider but when I contemplate, "are my straight coworkers being flirtatious or just friendly," I go from RN (registered nurse) to RC (really clueless) in 2.4 seconds.

Sometimes their come-ons have been subtle, a brush down the arm that lingers, disguised behind a ruse of feeling the difference between flannel and cashmere. One particular co-worker, however, is more bold. She once started a phone conversation by announcing, "I'm sitting naked in a vat of olive oil with cucumbers over the delicate parts." Despite the clearly suggestive nature of her comment, I dismissed it. Queer chicks know our private parts are not all that delicate. Just ask anyone who likes to be fisted.

When this same co-worker came into my office and sat on my lap, I was just confused. Later, I tried to explain the reason for my consternation but became embarrassed.

"That kind of thing," I stammered, "makes people talk."

"Let 'em talk," my co-worker answered. "They talked about Jesus Christ."

It's difficult to argue with the logic of a comment like that. Especially when the person making the comment accompanies it with a hearty lick to your forearm.

Still, I couldn't tell. Was she coming on to me? I rationalized, "No, because she's married." As if thousands of years of gay evolution hadn't proved how little that matters.

But I was still unsure, so I asked around. It turns out a bunch of other dykes, especially those who work in female dominated professions, have witnessed similar behavior at their jobs. Apparently where large numbers of women gather there are usually some straight women present (the WNBA being the obvious exception) and some of them have been known to flirt. So what is it? Does the free-floating estrogen force the straight women to make advances?

"It's not flirting exactly because they would never act on it," one lesbian explained to me. "It's not about sex, it's about relieving boredom."

The theory was confirmed earlier this year when I went with my coworkers to an out of state conference. One evening we decided to make a pilgrimage to a nearby hot springs. Despite the option of soaking in a spring-fed pool where we could wear our swim suits, my co-worker bought tickets for the clothing prohibited spring-filled caves.

As an American female (or whatever) I am required by federal law to have at least moderate body shame. I'm not exactly thrilled with stripping in front of my cat. I could have excused myself and gone to the clothing permissive haven of the pool, but I did not. I was not about to be outdone by the straight chicks. I gave myself a silent pep talk. "You can do this! You've been to three-day play parties! You've eaten tofu surprise made by women wearing less clothes than this." So before you could say, "swollen labia" there I was swimming. Naked. With my boss and flirtatious co-worker. In a cave.

This was the real test: would nakedness lead to true flirting and then perhaps to something more? I'm a hot-blooded woman (or whatever), I'm not above ogling other women (or whatevers) in practically any state of dress or undress. But as we eased in and out of the pools, naked and giggling, like a really bad scene from a very poorly executed girl-on-girl porno, I felt nothing, not even when my coworker laid on a bench and began doing hamstring stretches.

As I dressed, it came to me. The question was not, "Is my co-worker bored enough to put her clit where her mouth is" but, "Am I bored enough to put *my* mouth where her clit is?"

Judging from the lack of loin tingling action, apparently, the answer was no.

Widow Camp

I got a random email from someone whose grief blog I follow.

"Hi!" he said, by way of greeting. He went on to ask, with no other lead in, "So, are you going to Widow Camp."

Actually he said, "So are you going to Widow Camp?!" He was either very excited about Widow Camp, or he was using an emoticon with which I was unfamiliar. Maybe a question mark/exclamation point looks like a sideways face with an ironic grin.

A face that says, "I'm kidding about Widow Camp, or at the very least, I'm kidding about the name."

Neither the name nor his enthusiasm was made up. This guy, an older gay man who last year lost his partner of thirty-three years to pancreatic cancer, could not wait to go to Widow Camp.

He sent me the link, but before I could even peek, self-created images of what I could only imagine Widow Camp to be popped into my head.

I pictured forty widows on a converted school bus, which would be painted a slightly darker, more sedate hue, downgraded from the too bright and cheery yellow. The bus would have Widow Camp written on the side of the bus in a font that looked like the letters had been made of sticks nailed together.

People who are old enough to be widowed are probably too old to need to have their parents drop them off at the bus, so I expect that most of us would be dropped off by friends. Our friends would hand us our suitcase from the back of the car and would stand awkwardly while the rest of the widows piled onto the bus. We won't have all that much to load up, since the dress code will certainly be basic black.

They would all say, "well uh...have...uh..." and then there would be some more awkward silence while our friends realized they almost told us to "have fun" at Widow Camp. Instead, they'd hug us tightly and say "take care" which is American English for, "I'm really sorry about what you're going through and wish I could say something, anything, to make it better."

Once we were on the bus, an enthusiastic young counselor would say, "Welcome to Widow Camp!" really enjoying the alliteration of it, and then promptly start an appropriate Widow Camp icebreaker.

"Okay, turn to the person on your left and share the last the words your spouse said to you. And then turn to the person on your right and share your biggest regret about their death. Okay, ready. Go!"

And then there would be this excited rush of sharing and we'd all get so loud that the nineteen-year-old counselor would have to scold us. "Now quiet down now, you crazy widows!"

When we were done sharing last words/greatest regrets, the music counselor would stand up with a guitar and teach us the words to the Widow Camp theme song which would undoubtedly be set to the tune of Candle in the Wind and in which Elizabeth Kubler Ross would be rhymed not only with "loss" but also with "boss" and maybe even "moss." Because this is camp, after all. We'd then join together in some camp choruses, maybe, "If You're a Widow and You Know It Clap Your Hands."

When we got close to Widow Camp there would be a sign off the highway and we'd all explode with excitement and a spontaneous chant of WIDOW CAMP-WIDOW CAMP-WIDOW CAMP would break out. And we'd all stomp our feet to the words. *Widow Camp, Widow Camp.* As we pulled under the archway that says "Widow Camp: More Fun Than Crying At Home Alone."

But I wonder, will there be Widow Cliques? What if, for example, the 9/11 widows are totally tough and try and do panty raids on us while we're having Individual Crying Sessions? Will we have to stand up to them, saying, "Hey I'm a 6/17 widow and a 2/13 widow, so back up and also give me back my panties!"

Also, if I ever say "panties" to describe my underwear please come and rescue me because I will have been at Widow Camp way too long.

Our days will start with a lone bugle-playing reveille, followed by the greeting "Good morning WIDOW CAMP! Rise and, um, you may have noticed the person you love most in life is missing from your bed. So seriously, you might as well get up."

Most camps have cabin time clean up in the mornings with the awards for the tidiest cabins, but Widow Camp will have awards for the campers that pack their psychological baggage most neatly.

Then we'll head to our activities, like arts and crafts. At leatherwork, we'll make little lanyards to hold the mini ash urns we made in ceramics. And we'll make tissue out of birch bark.

In the evening, we'll all gather around a campfire, roast

S'mores of Sorrow and sing old Widow Camp favorites like Monty Python's "Always Look on the Bright Side of Death." When it gets dark, we'll huddle close and tell scary stories like, "My wife didn't have any life insurance" or "I had to fight my husband's parents to take him off the ventilator" or "Now I've got to raise the kids on my own."

But they will not play Taps before we all go to sleep, because, really we're all sad enough.

That's my fantasy about Widow Camp.

But then I checked the website, and from the videos it seems like a bunch of middle-aged women doing the Electric Slide.

Which isn't so different than what I had envisioned.

Everyone Cries On The A Train

What Doesn't Kill You Makes You Weirder, Part I
A.K.A. How To Lose The Love Of
Your Life & Still Be Funny

For best results, read this in a poetic monotone,
perhaps wearing a black beret.

Teardrops Keep Falling On My Head

We got bad news.
We were always getting bad news.
As was our custom, we went to bed to cry.
The phone rang, and as I changed position to answer it,
Heather accidentally clipped me with her elbow.
The force of the blow sent a tear into her ear, which had
slid off my cheek.
She jumped up and began shaking one leg, like a
swimmer trying to rid themselves of pool water.
"Do you think this situation is covered in the CDC
guidelines regarding exchange of body fluids?" She asks.
"No," I say, "I don't think they ever thought of this."

Everyone Says it's Hard to Get Rid of Jehovah's Witnesses

Everyone says it's hard to get rid of Jehovah Witnesses,
but that's not true.
Greet them at the door, and say
    Is this going to take long?
    My partner just got home from chemo
    and she's really sick.
It helps if you are carrying
a bucket of puke.

Hmmmm

The same drug company that makes the most potent—
and therefore most constipating—narcotic pain
medications also makes the most effective stool softeners.
Coincidence?
or just
exceptionally
good
marketing?

How To Get By

I get by writing Onion headlines in my head.
"Local woman manages intense emotional pain by watching
Bob Newhart reruns, eating Captain Crunch, and amusing
herself by sending gross weblinks to her friends."
What, you didn't enjoy the link to the pilonidal cyst site?
What? It's just a link.
No one said you had to click on it.

Portland Is Full of Hippies

The visitor to our house, an energy worker herself, tells
me that our cat Rosie is doing a lot of energy work for me,
and for Heather and for the house.
As if to prove the point, Rosie spends the next 45 minutes
licking his balls.
"energy work"

Tips for Hospice

When you have a patient—or a patient's family member—
on hold, you might think "A Whole New World" is a good
choice for background music.
It is not.
Nor is any Disney song.
Nor the soundtrack from the movie Beaches.

Planning the Funeral

Heather is the kind of person who wants every detail of
her funeral planned in advance. When we are finished,
I am crying.

She hugs me and says, "It will be no fun, when I'm done."

And then adds, "How's that for Dr. Suess meets Elizabeth
Kubler Ross?"

All These Tests

You know the dream you have, the dream where you're
panicking because you're at school and you have a test,
but you haven't been to class all semester?

I feel like that a lot.

Like all of life is a test I didn't study for.

Heather died at home, and once the hospice nurse
declared the death, I called the funeral director to come
pick her body up.

Three hours later they still hadn't showed.

I called again.

The funeral director said "Oh were you done
with the body?"

I stuttered. "What. We. Um. Oh. Um."

What were we supposed to be doing with the body?

My friend Stacy said "We kept expecting the grown ups to
show up."

Turns out we are the grown ups.

I Have the Raw Material For A Practical Joke But No Ideas For Completion

What am I supposed to do with all these Amnesty
International return address labels
emblazoned
with my dead lover's name?

Everyone Cries on the A Train

I cry a lot on the A train, but, I am noticing, so does everyone else.

I am an aggressive crier though.

If someone stares, I say, "What, ya never saw a bulldyke cry in public before?"

And then add, "Well stick around, because there's about 20 more minutes just like this."

I Am Visiting My Grief Counselor

I am visiting my grief counselor at the Cancer Resource Center. Her services are free because Heather died of cancer.

If Heather had been hit by a bus, I guess I would be paying out of pocket.

I am sobbing. For a very long time.

My grief counselor says, "It doesn't seem like you are having any trouble accessing your emotions."

Free or not, sometimes I want to punch my grief counselor in the head.

What Doesn't Kill You Makes You Weirder, Part II, A.K.A. How to Lose the Love of Your Life Twice and Still Be Funny

Family, Part One

The *Free to Be You and Me* album came out when I was four. I have no idea how a copy made it way into our house, but we were listening to the record on the turntable in our family room when my dad walked through.

The song that was playing was Rosey Grier singing "It's Alright to Cry."

My dad stopped short and looked at us.

"I hope no one's getting any fuckin' ideas around here."

We weren't.

Family, Part Two

When Cheryl got sick, I sent an email to my family letting them know. My brother wrote back immediately with an answer one could only get from someone who is career military.

"I was filled with regret when I read your email. It would seem like one situation of this type would be more than sufficient."

Yes indeed, my dear sweet brother, it would seem that way.

All This Irony

All of New York, it seems, is ironic. The key to being cool is that you can do more or less anything you want, as long as are you doing it ironically.

Oh these rips in my pants? Ironic.

This Lego tee shirt? Ironic.

Going to church? I'm doing it for the irony.

You know, I am forty-three and I've have had two girlfriends in a row die of the same disease, both just shy of their thirty-ninth birthdays.

Now that's irony, Mr. Polyester Leisure Suit on Top, Skinny Jeans on Bottom.

That's irony.

At the Dyke March

A week after Cheryl died, I went to the New York Dyke March.

I was sitting in Bryant Park waiting for it to start and an acquaintance said brightly, "Oh hey Kelli, where's Cheryl?'

I said "um, you didn't...

I mean...she passed away."

She scampered away.

Less than one minute later, another acquaintance stopped by.

She said brightly, "Hey Kelli, where's Cheryl?"

I was losing patience. "She's dead."

Acquaintance #2 responded "No not Heather, *Cheryl*"

I said "No, no um she died too."

Acquaintance #2 scampered away more quickly than Acquaintance #1.

I Start All My Comedy Sets

After my second partner in a row died, I start all my comedy sets with, "Life is short."

And then add, "Thank God!"

A friend, a comic, says "Wow that's a risky opening"

"I know," I say, "people laugh about 80 percent of the time."

My comic friend asks "What happens the other 20 percent of the time?"

I shrugged: "It kind of looks something like a cross between a cringe

and a wince. "

Shut Up and Be Devastated

It is Cheryl's birthday and she has been dead four months
but random people
(obviously people who don't really know her)
are wishing her happy birthday on her Facebook wall.
Not "Happy birthday Cheryl, we miss you" or
"Happy birthday Cheryl, hope you are at peace and having
a party wherever you are."
but "Hey Cheryl :) have a great day."
I get annoyed and start writing "she's dead" in response to
each such post.
This is an excellent use of my time.
A friend calls me and I rant at her for a while. I end with,
"I don't know what to do."
She yells, "Just be devastated! Be devastated! There's
nothing to do but shut up and be devastated."
That's actually not bad advice.
And to supplement feeling devastated, I also went to see a
movie.

Don't Diss My Affirmations

I have just one affirmation I am using at this time in my
life: "Just for today I will not lay down lie in the gutter and
die."
Not that this is really an option.
It's New York, after all, and someone will come along and
poke you with a stick.
Perhaps they will do it
ironically.

This Lone Blog

A few months after Heather died, I started posting all
my writing about her death and my grief onto a separate
blog I called Death Comedy Jam. At the time I wrote, "not

quite sure why I am keeping this all here."
Now that Cheryl died I look back at those posts
I am searching "How was I at one month? At two
months? At four?"
Oh, I see who I was keeping it for now.
I was keeping it for me.

Well That's Convenient

My sister wrote me a card the December after Heather
died.
It had a picture of the skaters at Rockefeller Center and
she wrote, "When you feel like it's always winter and
never Christmas in your heart, remember New York is a
great place to start over."
The December after Cheryl died, I got it out and put it up
on my bulletin board.
Recycling.
Yay.

I Hate This Tattoo

When I was in Haiti after the earthquake I was amazed by
how people, in the most dire of dire circumstances, would
say *lespa fe viv* — that is, "hope makes life."
I was so inspired by it I got a tattoo of those very words.
I grew to hate this tattoo after Cheryl died.
Oh, hope makes life? Really?
No, hope doesn't make life, but hope makes hope and
there are more choices once you've chosen hope.
I'm not sure if that's true or total bullshit, but for today, it's
keeping me off the Q train tracks.
That and Catholic guilt over leaving a
big mess
for someone else
to clean up.

Lulu The Cat Says 'Screw You'

Anyone who tells a lesbian couple cat story might logically be expected to include as least one other predominantly lesbian theme as well. For example, you might be anticipating a little subplot wherein we found out three weeks into our couples therapy that one or both of us had had sex with the therapist or at very least shared an ex.

We never did couples therapy.

You might expect to hear a story about how being a mixed status (vegetarian/meat-eater) couple caused us conflict. It did not cause us conflict. In fact, when I would walk out of the kitchen eating a bowl of just meat, my girlfriend Cheryl would observe "Wow, it's like living with a dinosaur," and then happily add, "Thank god you still have your incisors."

You might expect at least to hear a story about how we had sex and then immediately moved in together.

No. We lived in New York and we're middle aged. Rent control and putting your socks where you want is more important at this point than even the great and honored tradition of lesbian codependency.

In fact, it wasn't until Cheryl got sick with Hodgkin's lymphoma that we moved in together. It was an easy enough transition I suppose, except for one problem.

Cheryl had a cat named Lulu, a sweet Russian Blue who had her own mind about how things should go. I would decide I was going to sit on one side of the couch and she would wedge herself between me and my computer until I petted her or got up and left the couch entirely.

"Hey cat," I'd say, "You aren't the boss of me."

And Lulu the Cat said, "Screw you."

During the time Cheryl was on chemo, her white cells hit a devastating low. Her oncologist agreed to keep her out of the hospital but Cheryl couldn't go anywhere near the cat box. This meant I had to clean the cat box.

"The alternative no one is discussing," I muttered under my breath one day as I reluctantly scooped poo, "is the cat could go live somewhere else."

And Lulu the Cat said "Screw you."

Lulu would cuddle with me in bed with Cheryl, or when Cheryl was home. But on Saturday mornings when Cheryl made the trek into Manhattan to teach her writing class, Lulu would ignore me like it was her job.

"Hey cat," I'd say, trying to coax her out from under the bed, "just because I'm here and Cheryl isn't doesn't mean anything in particular. You see, she'll be here later."

But still, Lulu the Cat said "Screw you."

When Cheryl was hospitalized with a toxic pulmonary reaction to the chemo she had been given, I moved into the hospital with her. I would come home on Friday afternoons and pet Lulu and tell her everything would be okay.

"Just because I'm here and Cheryl isn't doesn't mean anything special, you'll see, she'll be here later." I would say, almost certainly believing this myself.

And Lulu the Cat said, "Screw you."

Cheryl got worse, then got better, and then got much worse again. In June of this past year, I came home to the apartment and put Lulu on my lap.

"Hey little cat dude, I seriously did the best I could. I'm sorry."

And Lulu the Cat said, "Fuck you."

I didn't want to sleep in our bed, but I didn't want Lulu to be alone, so after Cheryl died I attempted to spend nights on the living room couch. Lulu would stand on my chest and make an extremely annoying cat sound until I came and slept in the bed.

"Hey little cat dude," I would say, "I do not want to sleep in this bed without Cheryl here."

To which Lulu the Cat said, "Screw you."

Since Cheryl did not make any legal arrangements, everything went to her mom: her apartment, her money, her bills, and her body. I don't have even a tablespoon of Cheryl's ashes.

And I suppose Lulu should have by all rights gone to live with Cheryl's mom, but I told Cheryl's mom that wasn't happening. Lulu may not have liked me exactly, but I found a description that Cheryl has written about the time her mom owned a cat. Her mom's cat, Cheryl wrote, was exposed to so much second-smoke it had a little kitty smoker's cough.

"See what I'm saving you from, Lulu?" I whispered in her ear when we moved back to the Brooklyn queer group apartment I had called home before I moved in with Cheryl.

And Lulu the Cat said, "Screw you."

Up until this point, Lulu had only lived with the very orderly Cheryl in a very quiet house. Now she lived with me, two roommates, two other cats, and a huge dog. The first night at the new place, Lulu climbed onto my chest as I was falling asleep. "I'm sorry little cat dude," I said, "I did the very best I could. I'm sorry our little family is so small."

And Lulu the Cat, as she laid her head on my chest and fell asleep said, "Screw you."

Lulu is remarkably adjustable for a cat and she has learned to deal with the fact that sometimes I pile my hoodies on my bedroom chair, and sometimes I don't make my bed. In the beginning, both of these things bothered her very much. I still get a dirty look now, but she doesn't attempt to paw down the hoodies, or refuse to sleep on an unmade bed.

She sits on my lap pretty much every moment I am working and I will let her, and follows me around the apartment, even sometimes to the bathroom.

"I can't believe your inheritance from a lesbian relationship is a cat," my teenage nephew observed. "That's the most lesbian thing in the world."

For a while, every few weeks Cheryl's mom emailed me to inquire about Lulu.

I always ask My Little Gray Monster. "Hey cat dude do you want to go live in New Jersey and take up second-hand smoking?"

To which Lulu the Cat yawns, stretches herself further out on my lap and says, "Screw you."

Arrive Alive: The Fine Art of Family Holiday Survival

For more holidays than I can count without getting a nervous twitch in my eye, I made the Philadelphia to Daytona Beach trek with my older sister, her husband and their two kidlets. The trip, often in a compact car, led to the Florida house that my mom shared with her husband at the time, a retired army colonel everyone including my mom, referred to as The Colonel. The house was adorned with a wide assortment of dead animal skins on the floor and a number of historically significant weapons on the walls. It was a fun place.

As we snaked down Interstate 95, past billboards for a Noted South Carolina Racist Attraction and others advertising "Carnivore Heaven Bar and Grill," or "Agorama: The World's First Agricultural Theme Park," I would find myself sweating more with each passing mile. I would crane my head out the car window, scanning the highways for rainbow bumper stickers or any sign of Queer Life and repeat my mantra:

I can survive the holidays with my family.

I can survive the holidays with my family.

Many years and thousands of dollars of therapy later, I fancy myself a bit of an expert in the "let's wrestle some fun out of this dysfunction" arena. And despite the warnings of my friends, therapist(s), exes and perhaps even my pets, I still spend winter holidays with my huge, alcoholic family of origin. I have tools now though, so don't try this at home. If you absolutely must try it at home, be sure to observe these important survival guidelines to decrease the statistical likelihood of family gatherings ending with tears or blood being shed.

As much as possible, avoid the more intense family interactions like group meals. These can be a breeding ground for cutlery mishaps, eating disorder relapses and semi-drunken brawls. Taking a job such as firefighter, emergency medical technician, undertaker or nurse practically guarantees that you can always use the excuse, "I'm so sorry I can't make it but [sigh] I have to work." If your family insists on having holiday meals locally to accommodate your oh-so-busy schedule, clip your little cousin's walkie talkie to your belt and explain you're "on call." Run out right after the turkey is served.

If you're not able to excuse yourself, at the very least avoid coming out to your family in the midst of holiday meals. At least not *spontaneously*. That rush of warmth you thought you felt could just be heartburn from your aunt Sophie's bacon and pepperoni dressing. The resulting indigestion you might experience would probably not be life-threatening, but could indeed feel like it.

You can also feign intestinal disorder that requires constant trips to the bathrooms. This is a fail-safe way of avoiding troublesome, boring or even insulting topics of conversation. For example, for many years, every time my family gathered, my grandmother liked to tell the story about how lucky she was to have survived her bout with cancer, since the disease was caught at such a late stage.

"I didn't go to the doctor right away about the pain in my side," my grandma would explain, "because I thought

I was just sore from carrying Kelli around. She was such a big fat baby."

Silence.

"Hey," my grandma would say, "where's Kelli?"

Flush.

You get the picture.

It's also important to anticipate the end of a conversation before you initiate it. One year I asked The Colonel over pumpkin pie if the bayonets mounted on the living room wall were real. "For chrisskaes yes," he exclaimed, "what good is a bayonet if it's never been used to kill anyone?"

I learned something very important that day. If you can't handle the answer, don't ask the question.

The corollary to above mentioned rule is plan family-friendly conversational topics in advance. For example, I have a slight suspicion my mother won't want to hear about my accidental three-way at Atlanta Pride, but I'm sure she'll love my stories about discovering drag culture in rural Wisconsin. Write these safe conversational topics on an index card if you can't commit them to memory.

Yes, it's a little awkward to recite "Colonel, would you like to chat about the win to loss ratio of [insert name here], a local sports team?" But if the alternative is chatting about "those damn [insert name of ethnic group/random liberal group/ endangered species]," it's worth both the awkwardness and the effort. It's a documented fact that the average homosexual can listen to only a limited number of anti-harp seal diatribes before going completely bananas.

Work with the family denial system, not against it. Remember what you learned from the friendly neighborhood dyke lifeguard? If you're caught in a rip tide, don't try to swim out of it. The riptide is always stronger than you are, and you'll tire yourself out before you can reach the beach. Swim parallel to a riptide. At some point a topographical feature on the shore will cause its strength to ebb and you'll be able to break away.

The same principle applies when dealing with what could be called a "reduced truth" family situation. Some may call a sideways confrontation passive aggressive, but I call it efficient.

Perhaps an example would prove instructive here. My mom had a tubal ligation nineteen months before I was born. In the 60's, the tubal ligation procedure involved only the clamping of the fallopian tubes, rather than actually severing them.

My brother, thinking I was already aware of this fact, mention it offhandedly at a Christmas gathering the year I turned thirty. I did some quick Internet research.

According to a CDC report done over a ten year period from 1965 until 1975, 365 post-tubal ligation women the CDC studied, 143 became pregnant at least once after the procedure. In other words, 1 in 155 tubal ligations were unsuccessful.

It seemed strange my mom had never mentioned my special status as a 1 in 155er. We weren't a timid clan by any stretch of the imagination. One of the explicitly stated family rules was, "Remember kids, we don't give each other the finger in front of grandma." My biological father was of the genre of dads that thought great fun on a road trip involved farting and then locking the windows of the family station wagon.

I couldn't understand the silence over this simple medical fact.

I decided to chat with my mom about this. The day after Christmas, I accompanied her on an early morning drive to pick up donuts for all the visiting relatives. I had only managed to say, "Mom, you could have told me about the tubal lig—" before my mom turned the steering wheel sharply to the right while simultaneously hitting the brakes.

This sent the car skidding onto the gravel shoulder.

"I can't believe how close that car came to hitting us," she said, genuinely breathless.

It was 7 a.m. on a Saturday morning and we were driving on a deserted stretch of highway in rural Florida. There was no traffic for miles.

I nodded and agreed that, indeed, who could believe how close that car came to hitting us.

I can guess my mom's motivation for not wanting me to know that she had tried very hard to prevent my birth. She was worried that if I knew the truth it would shatter my self-esteem. On the contrary, knowing the truth resolved a lot of questions I had, most notably, "Why did my parents have one more kid?" Also, knowing that I was a direct result of a super fierce-ass egg fighting its way through a banded fallopian tube filled me with indescribable joy. It's like being born with a protest sign in hand: "I AM here! And I AM queer! Guess we're all going to have to get used to it!"

All the same I couldn't resist tormenting my mother about this absurd situation just a bit. The next Christmas I got my mom a special gift: a t-shirt I had sent to her house directly from the Planned Parenthood website. It was adorned with a picture of a smiling cartoon uterus and said simply, "Ask me about my tubal ligation."

See? Navigate within the confines of the family denial system, not against it.

Of course, if you're bringing your partner along to spend some quality time with your family of origin, the ordeal becomes more complicated. Positive outcomes, however, are not impossible.

Some tips:

Avoid doing the very first introduction of a new partner at a holiday gathering where there is no easy escape in case of backfire. Family vacations might be okay, if you're going down the shore and can join the traveling carnival set up by the boardwalk if things get really out of control. If you're planning a winter Pocono weekend trip with your entire extended family, a single snowstorm could throw the whole interaction deep into the unmanageable zone.

Process closet issues before, not during, the family get together. No, I don't mean a long discussion about the virtues of cedar paneling versus mothballs or a campy reenactment of the "no more wire hangers" scene from *Mommie Dearest*. I'm merely saying that if your partner is going to be introduced as "friend," "roommate," "personal trainer," "pal" or other such euphemism, they should know in advance.

Warn your partner—if you so desire—about the little eccentricities of your family, but don't expect to have warned them about the right things. For example, because I am both a registered nurse and a registered worrywart, I am known amongst my friends as "Safety Monitor Dyke." I was frequently (and inexplicably) the only person who brought a fire extinguisher to the Lesbian Avengers' flame eating demonstrations.

One Christmas my partner watched my cousins (who had each polished off a six pack of Old Milwaukee) head into the woods, chainsaws and axes in hand. She turned to me with a stunned expression "what are they doing?" I replied, "chopping firewood, I guess." She was completely horrified by this blatant affront to personal safety, but I was completely accustomed to it.

Try to respect your partner's view of your family. Their objectivity may shed light into some very dark corners. For example, in the past ten years I have been involved in many useless arguments about the souls of cartoon characters. This is because at some point during every holiday gathering, my oldest sister authoritatively announces, "Smurfs are a satanic force from hell."

"No," I said, "the Smurfs are merely annoying. There is no evidence they are a satanic force from hell."

After this heated exchange one year, my partner asked if I might "perhaps choose battles a little more wisely?" And it's true, there is only so much reality you can interject into any given conversation. Although I was initially resistant, I realized she did have a point. After all, who appointed me Executive Director of the Cartoon Characters Defense League? Nowadays, I let the little blue bastards take care of themselves.

Unless you were raised by Seventh Day Adventists or the Krishnas, take your vegetarian partner out to eat before every family meal. As far as I can tell, my family seldom, if ever, encounter living, breathing vegetarians in their natural habitat, and this is why they don't truly understand vegetarian dietary habits. Or at least that's what I told my vegan partner when they offered her a humongous platter of turkey, explaining, "It's okay, we took out the bones, so it doesn't look like meat."

Refrain from responding to your partner's requests to pass the mashed potatoes with "Yes Mistress." Especially, if you would normally do so within the privacy of your own home.

Just trust me on this one.

If all else fails, remember that cheerfulness is an effective weapon in trained hands. My "Smurfs are Satan" sister has a ten-year-old daughter who at one point in her childhood came into the house crying after the neighborhood kids teased her. It seems that my niece had revealed that the only CD she had ever listened to was *Sandi Patty's Bible Memory Songs*. Faster than you can say, "put another fifty bucks in the therapy fund," my sister comforted her daughter with,

"The Bible says the world will hate Christians. Isn't it wonderful to be hated as Jesus was?"

Do you think my sister wants to know that I (the heathen sodomite) and my homosexually evil partner are actually happier than she is? No way. Sometimes collective cheesy grins (even if you have been thirty seconds away from homo-homicide for the last six months) can go a long way towards maintaining your collective sanity at holiday gatherings.

Finally, always plan an after-holiday holiday. Invite your queerest friends to your queer house for completely queer decompression. This might involve eating hummus and completing rainbow crafts. At the very least, everyone should wear a vest and sing a showtune or Holly Near song.

Think about scheduling a double session with your couple's therapist. And definitely plan on having the bill sent to your parents.

The Tragicomic Odyssey

A.K.A. The Year I Stopped Getting Invited to Parties

KELLI: My name is Kelli Dunham. I am a very funny stand up comic.

RANDOM PARTY GOER: I know who you are Kelli Dunham. I am approaching you in this social situation because stand up comics often make humorous comments in casual conversation. My life is hard sometimes and I was hoping you would make me laugh. Also I would like to engage in vaguely flirtatious banter with you because of your status as a Z list celebrity in the LGBT community. Meaning, of course, you have many friends on Facebook but no significant TV credits.

KELLI: My name is Kelli Dunham. I am a very funny stand up comic. 200,000 people died in the January 2010 earthquake in Haiti.

RANDOM PARTY GOER: (SILENCE) I am approaching you in this social situation because stand up comics often make humorous comments in casual conversation. My life is hard sometimes and I was hoping you would make me laugh.

KELLI: My name is Kelli Dunham. I am a very funny stand up comic. My girlfriend was diagnosed with cancer last November.

RANDOM PARTY GOER: (SILENCE, GLANCING UNEASILY FROM SIDE TO SIDE) I am approaching you in this social situation because stand up comics often make humorous comments in casual conversation. My life is hard sometimes and I was hoping you would make me laugh.

KELLI: My name is Kelli Dunham. I am a very funny stand up comic. Eighty-five percent of people with the type of cancer my girlfriend had are completely cured by chemotherapy. My girlfriend developed a reaction to the chemotherapy and died.

RANDOM PARTY GOER: (LONG SILENCE) I am approaching you in this social situation because stand up comics often make humorous comments in casual conversation. My life is hard sometimes and I was hoping you would make me laugh.

KELLI: My name is Kelli Dunham. I am a very funny stand up comic. Most people are saved by chemotherapy, but my girlfriend died because of it.

RANDOM PARTY GOER: (SILENCE)

KELLI: Sometimes people find irony humorous.

RANDOM PARTY GOER: (SILENCE, THEN THE SOUND OF CRICKETS)

KELLI: My name is Kelli Dunham. I am a very funny stand up comic. Thanks to the lawless military industrial complex, our environment is very toxic and dangerous. My last girlfriend also had cancer.

RANDOM PARTY GOER: (SILENCE) I am approaching you in this social situation because stand up comics often make humorous comments in casual conversation. My life is hard sometimes and I was hoping you would make me laugh.

KELLI: My name is Kelli Dunham. I am a very funny stand up comic. My last girlfriend also died. She used the assisted suicide provisions of the Oregon law to take her own life because she was in intractable anguish.

RANDOM PARTY GOER: (SILENCE)

KELLI: I called my most recent girlfriend my miracle love because I thought I would never love anyone after my other girlfriend died. She developed, and then died from the same disease my first girlfriend had. Having two partners who die of cancer within a five-year period is an extremely statistically unlikely negative situation, which is kind of the opposite of the concept of a miracle.

RANDOM PARTY GOER: (VERY LONG SILENCE)

KELLI: Sometimes people find irony humorous.

RANDOM PARTY GOER: (VERY LONG SILENCE)

KELLI: My name is Kelli Dunham. I am a very funny stand up comic. I have a friend who was trapped for six days in a collapsed building after the earthquake in Haiti in January 2010.

RANDOM PARTY GOER: (SILENCE)

KELLI: Both her feet had to be amputated because of the substandard medical care she received in a field hospital operated by the United Nations.

RANDOM PARTY GOER: (SILENCE)

KELLI: My name is Kelli Dunham. I am a very funny stand up comic. Have you ever seen maggots in an open wound?

RANDOM PARTY GOER: (SILENCE)

KELLI: I did not mean that as a rhetorical question.

RANDOM PARTY GOER: I just remembered I have something important I need to go do.

KELLI: I am sorry your life is hard sometimes. (PAUSE) I hope I have made you laugh.

RANDOM PARTY GOER: I just remembered I have something important I need to go do.

KELLI: My name is Kelli Dunham. I am a very funny stand up comic. Hey where are you going?

Acknowledgements

A few months ago I was using the bathroom at the small venue where I had just finished performing. While I was doing my business, I could hear two audience members unaware of my presence a few stalls over discussing the merits of the show. I didn't have much time to bask in the glow of their praise before I heard a third voice, which I recognized as belonging to the partner of a friend.

"Oh sure she's funny on stage," I heard the voice say above the sounds of toilet flushing and running water, "but ask her to a dinner party and I can guarantee she'll bring up the Haiti earthquake at least three times."

I huddled on the toilet for a few moments of silent indignation and thought about making a dramatic stomping exit scene. But then I remembered the conversational topics I introduced at the last couple of parties I'd been to, and I realized the assessment of my social presence was not just accurate, it was also charitable.

Fortunately I have really good friends who have come to accept not only my conversational limitations but also the limitations of my judgment. When your life is a series of Tales of Extreme Enthusiasm and Too Much Self Esteem, you make your friends worry about you, and I appreciate the patience of my friends who helped not only with the writing of this book, but with the surviving of the stories therein as well.

Thanks to:

My best friend, Maura "Poopyhead" Kelly, who has been present for many of these stories, once inspired me to get a revenge tattoo and has been known to make inappropriate jokes on airplanes.

My family, who has been extraordinarily good sports about being the primary subject of my comedy, especially in the very early years. The names of most of my siblings have been changed, but not drastically or consistently because I don't have a very good memory. Big thanks to Beth, Wes and Vi who have been the most consistent providers of material and support.

My mom, who will undoubtedly disagree with the truthiness of some of what is written here but since this is not presented as a historical family treatise, I also know she'll eventually be thrilled to be such a big part of my big queer book. Thanks for raising us to be a bunch of unruly individuals and letting me wear whatever I wanted to school.

The Missionaries of Charity in Miami, Delmas 31, Sans Fil, especially Sister Mira and Sister Madga, as well as my group sisters, the very kind Sister Sylvia (RIP) and the trying to be kind Sister Angeles. No thanks at all to the very nasty Sister Kateri. I know you're not supposed to say rotten things about dead people, but she was one mean nun. I'm also especially grateful to the friends and others who put up with me in those weird years in between Haiti and joining the convent, Rose Anderson and Cheryl Little especially.

LadyBeth and Johanna and the rest of the Catholic Worker Free Clinic gang, folks at Camp Echoing Hills who supported me my first year in Haiti, the kids at Lekol St. Vincent (email me guys!), John and Jodie Ackerman, Laura Coe, Howell Gieb III wherever you are, Dr Rich, Koleta and Roger Stamper, Joanne Kischuck now known as Sister John Marie and everyone at Heartline.

Everyone who was present at *Pudding Day* and continues to be an important part of my life, thanks for your support and love. Thanks to Barbara Buckley, Stacy Bias, Barbara Carellas, and Kate Bornstein who have been supporters of making *Pudding Day* the Day into *Pudding Day* the Play.

I also so appreciate my many long-time friends, too many to list here, who put me back together after not one but two partner deaths, as well as the Lovetroopers, Cheryl's friends who became my friends, and Genne Murphy who helped me heal both professionally through Queer Memoir and personally with her big heart. Thanks to my eight million therapists, Friends Indeed, LCI, Palliative Care at BIMC, and my grief pals Kelly, Marc and Cami. Thanks also to Sarah Schulman for the beautiful words "shut up and be devastated," for being a champion of consistency and for kicking my ass when it needs kicking. Thanks also to Staci Priano for your help during that time as well as special thanks to Lea Robinson. Lea knows why.

Thanks to the Fresh Fruit Festival where *Bad Habit* first debuted in New York, as well as Dale Sorenson who took the script places I never imagined it could go.

Thanks also to all the event producers who have made the last decade of shows possible: folks who put together my southern tour, pride directors, kids at colleges, and everyone who provided Diet Mountain Dew or hospitality or rides to and from the airport.

I also greatly appreciate the input of my writers' group Luisa, Anne, and Virginia although if there is anything stupid or horrible in here, it's not their fault.

A big huge thanks to Tom and Julie of Topside, who are changing the world one beautiful cover design and one success-bullying incident at a time.

Finally, I guess it's pretty stupid to acknowledge dead people in a book intro but just in case they're reading this, here goes. A big huge thank you to two of the loves of my life, Cheryl Burke and Heather MacAllister and to my grandma Viola St. Clair who prayed for me every night that I would find "the perfect will of God for my life."

I don't know if queer stand-up comic was the outcome you were envisioning, Grandma, but it seems pretty perfect to me.

About the Author

KELLI DUNHAM is an award-winning stand-up comic who has appeared on both Showtime and the Discovery Channel and tours nationally to colleges, comedy clubs, LGBT pride events and even the occasional livestock auction. Her comedy albums *I am NOT a 12 Year Old Boy, Almost Pretty*, and *Why Is the Fat One Always Angry* are in regular rotation on Sirius/XM radio's Rawdog Comedy as well as Pandora's Margaret Cho station. An ex-nun, and a current registered nurse, Dunham's previous titles have included *How to Survive and Maybe Even Love Nursing School* (FA Davis, 2005) and *How to Survive and Maybe Even Love Your Life as a Nurse* (FA Davis, 2006) have sold over 100,000 copies.

Freak of Nurture is her fifth book.

OTHER TITLES AVAILABLE **NOW**
from **TOPSIDE PRESS + TOPSIDE SIGNATURE**

THE COLLECTION
Short Fiction from the Transgender Vanguard
edited by *Tom Léger & Riley MacLeod*

A dynamic composite of rising stars, **The Collection** represents the depth and range of tomorrow's finest writers chronicling transgender narratives. 28 authors from North America converge in a single volume to showcase the future of trans literature and the next great movements in queer art.

19.95 paperback • 32.95 hardcover

MY AWESOME PLACE
The Autobiography of Cheryl B
written by *Cheryl Burke*

A rare authentic glimpse into the electrifying arts scene of New York City's East Village during the vibrant 1990s, **My Awesome Place** is the chronicle of a movement through the eyes of one young woman working to cultivate her voice while making peace with her difficult and often abusive family.

An unlikely story for someone whose guidance counselor recommended a career as a toll taker on the New Jersey Turnpike, Burke was determined to escape her circumstances by any means available–physical, intellectual or psychotropic. Her rise to prominence as the spoken word artist known as Cheryl B brought with it a series of destructive girlfriends and boyfriends and a dependence on drugs and alcohol that would take nearly a decade to shake.15.95 paperback • 25.95 hardcover

NEVADA
a novel by *Imogen Binnie*

Nevada is the darkly comedic story of Maria Griffiths, a young trans woman living in New York City and trying to stay true to her punk values while working retail. When she finds out her girlfriend has lied to her, the world she thought she'd carefully built for herself begins to unravel, and Maria sets out on a journey that will most certainly change her forever.

17.95 paperback • 29.95 hardcover

UPCOMING RELEASES
from TOPSIDE PRESS + TOPSIDE SIGNATURE

BRIGHT LIKE NEON
a novel by *Angelina Anderson* • Fall 2013

Bright Like Neon follows the story of Jody Louden, a 17-year-old aspiring roller derby star and her first crush on a girl–the DJ at the roller rink, of course. When one of the white girls at her private school goes missing, Jody and her friends are forced to reckon with adulthood sooner than any of them had planned.

READY, AMY, FIRE
a novel by *Red Durkin* • Fall 2013

Hans Tronsmon is an average 20 year-old transgender man. He's the popular chair of the transmasculine caucus at his women's college and the first draft of his memoir is almost finished. But his world is turned upside down when his happily married gay dads decide to stop paying for his off-campus apartment and start saving for retirement. Hans must learn to navigate the world of part-time jobs, publishing, and packers if he wants to survive. *Ready, Amy, Fire* is the harrowing tale of one man's courageous journey into boyhood.

MORE INFO: TOPSIDEPRESS.COM
STORE.TOPSIDEPRESS.COM